Tablets of
EMOTIONAL WISDOM

GOPI NAIR

BALBOA.PRESS
A DIVISION OF HAY HOUSE

Balboa Press books may be ordered through booksellers or by contacting:

Balboa Press
A Division of Hay House
1663 Liberty Drive
Bloomington, IN 47403
www.balboapress.com
1 (877) 407-4847

Print information available on the last page.

ISBN: 978-1-9822-4050-9 (sc)
ISBN: 978-1-9822-4049-3 (hc)
ISBN: 978-1-9822-4051-6 (e)

Library of Congress Control Number: 2019921101

Balboa Press rev. date: 12/23/2019

Contents

How Do You Know If Your Wife Loves You?

If your wife criticizes you, it is a sign that she loves you very much and more! If she asks you to do more chores around the house, it means she sees your hidden potential. If she complains that you are not making enough, it is an indication that your talents are wasted! If she unleashes her desires, she is opening doors—for you to do more and become the best man around. Use emotional wisdom to dissect criticism. And stop reacting to what others are saying. Your wife is probably the person closest to you. She alone knows your strengths and weaknesses. Why is she not praising or complimenting? She does not want you to be complacent. To draw lessons for your personal growth, be a keen listener; listen to her comments closely! Then train your mind to act instead of react. When you use your emotional wisdom to evaluate, when you are in earnest about being the best, then negative comments become music to your ears!

You Are the Light of the World!

"You are the light of the world," proclaims the Bible. Why
are you the light of the world? You are the dispeller of the
darkness of ignorance! *"Aham brahmasmi,"* proclaims Hindu
scriptures—"Every human is a potential divine," an heir apparent
to almighty God, the creator, who made you in his image.
The purpose of life is to seek truth, our identities. *Who
am I? Why am I here? What is my purpose?* Asking
these questions basically alters our paradigms. A
paradigm shift is essential for transformation.
We are not here just to eat, sleep, and reproduce. Humanity is the
greatest creation on planet Earth. You are a lion but think you are
a simple donkey! Alter your thoughts; think like a lion, and roar!
You are made in the image and likeness of God; you
were born to win, succeed, and make a difference. A
simple awareness that you are here for a purpose is all
that you need to shine as the light of the world.

What Is Fate in Life?

In many cultures, we talk about fate. Is there somet ...g
called *fate* in life? Fate is spelled *f-a-t-e, fruit ate*—
we have to eat the fruit of our actions.
Even innocent children have to eat the fruit. If they put their
hands in the fire, their hands will be burned. So parents protect
their children from fire. As adults, we are our own protectors.
The law of karma says the same thing, in essence. If you
sow the seeds of oranges, you cannot reap apples. If you
do good deeds, only good can come out of it, whatever
you sow. "Only what you sow can you reap" is law.
What is the way out of fate? What can you do? Repent;
seek forgiveness from those you have hurt! Plant
healing thoughts in your mind, and try to help with
divine grace. You shall say goodbye to old fate.
Understanding the law of fate is half the battle. Creating
a new fate is well within your reach and control. Start
sowing the seeds of a new fate, seeds of gratitude—the
spiritual catalyst that can bring true joy into your life.

Emotional Hygiene—
How to Practice It

Emotional hygiene is essential for emotional health.
Emotional health is as important as physical health.
Understanding emotions is the basis of emotional hygiene.
You can even produce emotions to learn from them.
External factors—such as an accident or somebody's speech or
action—cause those emotions. Emotion is really intense energy
movement. Here, I refer to thought energy as *intense movement*.
Anger, fear, and grief are three basic negative emotions.
Love, compassion, kindness, and gratitude are positive.
Different people manage their emotions differently
based on culture, upbringing, and personal traits.
You can calculate your vulnerability to situations and prepare
yourself to deal with them effectively. Anybody can react to a
situation and be a victim of a resulting outburst of violent emotions.
Emotional hygiene involves an acute awareness that you
are the master of your emotions. You can be in control
by understanding the nature of your emotions; you can
learn to manage every situation through practice.
Don't wait until your house is on fire to seek a fire
extinguisher. Practice emotional hygiene every day. Cultivating
positive emotions like love, compassion, and gratitude
is the best practice to overcome negative emotions.

There Are No Accidents in the Universe!

You are on purpose! The universe is on purpose! There are no
accidents in the universe! Accept all the events that take place in
your life. Analyze every event, learn the lesson, and move on.
Every experience, better or bitter, is a teacher appointed by the
universe to deliver a message. Read and internalize the message in
its spirit, knowing full well that the experience was meant to be so.
Life blesses those souls who accept whatever comes,
abstain from blaming others, and avoid wasting energy.
Instead, embrace the adversity, and look for the clue
that is hidden as a message for you to learn from.
It is said that "every adversity carries in it a fertile seed"
capable of producing greatness if pursued with vigor.
Looking back at one's own life, one can see tiny dots that,
when connected, complete the life's pivotal message.

Change and Personal Transformation

Change happens; it is a function of time. Transformation is the
result of conscious efforts. Time is the author of change; the mind
is the author of conscious transformation. It is defined destiny.
Change management is a misnomer; change simply happens!
There is nothing to manage; change is purely accidental. A
forest, which is full of unintended growth, can be compared to
change, whereas a beautiful garden is like transformation.
Intense desire is the basis of transformation. If you build
on that desire with training, rituals, and new attitudes and
philosophies, you become a new person, a transformed being!
Is it easy to transform oneself? Of course not! It
involves daily sacrifices, unmatched perseverance,
and sheer hard work supported by a conviction. The
result: a new person, ready to change the world!

Is Fear of Death Fear of the Unknown?

Death is a totally unknown phenomenon. How can you be afraid of something unknown? Is it fear of the total loss of everything known? This is something everyone needs to ponder. We all know that we have lots of possessions and many attachments to our spouses and children, parents, brothers and sisters, and many close friends. Loss of attachments causes painful agony. Poets describe the phenomenon of death as the "sleep"— *mahanidra*, the great sleep from which there is no coming back. When the energy that powers the body is withdrawn, the organism stops functioning, and the body is lifeless. Should you be afraid of death and let fear paralyze you? Mother Nature has planned our lives so well that no one needs to worry about death anymore. Time prepares us to face the end of time in peace. As every day goes by, we are nearing the end of life. And as we age, we internalize the ultimate truth of death. As people we grew up with, with whom we spent life, slowly start departing, we know our times are also nearing.

Yes! We Are All Connected!

We are all connected at the spiritual level. Being part of the universe is natural. It goes deeper. Stop thinking behind the backs of other people; they will get your thought vibrations. Always act as if the person you're thinking about is sitting next to you. And think only good things about him or her. You can use this communication mode many times; it is very effective at the subconscious level. Basically, you cannot hide your inner thoughts. They are things and very powerful spiritual chips. Sometimes you may feel uneasy in a person's presence, although you have no apparent reason to feel bad. Speak good of everyone; think noble thoughts. Thinking is a habit like brushing your teeth. What should you do if negative thoughts arise? Forgive yourself; seek forgiveness from the other. The web of spirituality spreads far and wide. And we are part of that spiritual web or network. Whenever verbal communication is lost in the noise, you can communicate effectively at the substratum level. Tapping into your own emotional wisdom is the key to managing thoughts, speech, and actions. This will teach you to speak the truth without hurting anyone. Always say what you mean and mean what you say.

Can Anybody Insult You without Your Permission?

Do you think anybody can insult you? Is your self-esteem so low as to allow that? Have you seen a dog barking at the moon? Receiving an insult is the best way to test your emotional wisdom. Do not fall for the paper tiger—another's opinion. Anybody can yell and shout and hurl bad words. But how you process such words is up to you. Let empty words and insults fall on deaf ears. There is no time to waste on others' opinions. Keep your self-esteem intact. And do your thing. Stay focused on the opinions of those who matter, and abandon the words of doubting Thomases. You are on purpose; the world is on purpose. Keep doing the things that you do very well. Let fools pay attention to the negativity-mongers. Do not give permission to anybody to insult you. You were born to win. You were born to succeed. Yes! You were born to make a difference in the world. Master emotional wisdom; stop reacting to others. Act like a master. You are the parent of your creativity.

How Are You Processing Data?

We receive and process volumes of data daily. Most of
the time, we process this information with bias and fear,
and the outcome can hurt and, at times, paralyze. Our
quality of life depends on how we process data.
Data by itself is harmless and inanimate, powerless. When it
is mixed with our fear, negativity, or other disabling emotions,
we lose! We lose our ability to look at the prime data as it is.
When a dear one gets sick and you get the information,
your unprepared mind starts processing the data:
What if? What if? and *What if?* and very seldom *What
if not?* Our wild imaginations color the data.
Thus, we look at our inner fears reflected! In that data, we receive
and jump to conclusions. This is where emotional wisdom helps
as a guide, and you evaluate the data without bias or fear.
Thus, you train your mind in emotional wisdom, and
you can handle any situation with positivity! This
will empower you to find a rational solution!

A New Year's Resolution for Everybody

As we stand on the eve of the New Year, we all can make
one New Year's resolution. It is easy, inexpensive, yet
priceless—that is just thirty minutes of exercise every day!
Regular exercise is a good cure for daily stress! It can keep your
blood pressure in check! It is good for your body and even better
for your mind—the best way to spend thirty minutes daily!
You can do fifteen minutes in the morning and the remaining
fifteen minutes after your work! You can do brisk walking, jogging,
or cycling. Raising your heart rate supports healthy living!
This helps create an awareness in your children, and
they will likely begin to exercise at a young age! This
is the best advice you can give to the young ones;
teaching by example is the backbone of parenting!
Thirty minutes of exercise can change your mood! It can promote
digestion and induce sound sleep! You will soon get addicted to
the endorphins, the body's feel-good hormones and painkillers!
Go ahead; make a New Year's resolution to exercise—
the best New Year's present for all your loved ones!
There is a hidden magic in starting anything new! You
will discover new opportunities in doing so!

Seven Ways to Use Emotional Wisdom

1. Start acting, and stop reacting!
2. Practice gratitude! Make it your only attitude!
3. When emotions run high, keep your mouth shut!
4. Be a keen listener! Talk less, and pay attention!
5. Learn and study more about your mind and its power!
6. Practice silence for a few minutes every day!
7. Develop a passion for life! Learn to do more!
"When your emotional knowledge is baked in the fire of life's experience, emotional wisdom is born!"

Carry Your Own Sunshine
Wherever You Go!

Once, certain creatures complained to the sun, "There is
a place in the universe immersed in darkness!" "I've never
heard of such a place. I ought to see that!" the sun responded.
Led by the creatures, the sun went to the darkest spot!
What happened? All the darkness simply vanished!
The sun basically erased all the darkness in the area!
We all can carry our own sunlight wherever we go!
Make a difference with a smile or a kind word!
Where there is darkness, shed some light! Even lighting a candle
will erase tons of darkness! Where there is hatred, bring a
little compassion! Where there is agony, bring some solace!
Rather than wasting time on the who and why, simply act to wipe
the tears of the helpless victim! A few acts of kindness we all can
do every day! There are small things that make a big difference!
Who says one man cannot make a difference? Rome was not built
in a day—nor the Tower of London! You and I can create that one-
person army, determined to make a difference, carrying sunlight!

Slow Down; It Is Your Lovely Life!

Slow down; it is your lovely life! Just like you relish one
morsel of rice, you need to relish life moment to moment!
Live in the present moment and there alone!
Your past is buried in lurking pain! And your future is filled
with gripping fears! The present is where you have to experience
joy—that feeling of contentment that you need more of!
Haste makes waste, with life slipping through your fingers as
though you were dead or dormant! Awareness is awesome! It is
eternally awake, feeling the very pulse of the present moment!
Herein hides the secret of perennial joy and mirth!
It is a timeless experience, unscattered by thoughts!
Thoughts wait for the moments to linger, as if they
are in an intimate embrace with the divine!
Slow down, my friend. Choose to relish moments. Do not run away
from the lasting joy in life! Attend to every moment as though it is
the last! If it is not, go down on your knees, and say, "Thank you!"

Do You Glorify the Work You Do?

Work is the repeated actions one does with the objective
of a certain purpose! You bring your talents and
character to accomplish various tasks involved!
You bring your "personal factor and glorify!" No job title can
glorify you! The reverse is true! Whatever work you do, you can
make it special! Glorify it; make it outstanding, even immortal!
One should not look at a job as an earning machine! It is beyond
the title, beyond the paycheck! A mere stonecutter becomes a
sculptor, an artist; paints a picture; becomes adorably famous!
You envision the outcome of your labor to last long enough to cover
generations after you! It is your gift to humankind in its hour of
need! It brings unspeakable peace and solace to seeking hearts!
Life gives all of us an opportunity to be a giver of gifts;
an opportunity to leave "our footprints in the sands"; a
timeless era to remind us of our eternal connection; a living
memory that we, too, were travelers on this little planet!
Open your heart, broaden your vision, and pour your
passion into whatever work you do, small or big or OK! You
have the opportunity to glorify it for others to enjoy! Leave
your fingerprints, even an enviable touch of greatness!

Change Your Thoughts, Change Your Life!

We all live in a world created by our thoughts! Thoughts are things; they carry great potential! We often complain about our life of misery! Yet we seldom realize that we sowed those seeds! "Everything multiplies after its kind" is universal! It is an inviolable law of the universe! Examine the thoughts that you entertain, though they percolate in the incubator of your mind! "As above, so below; as within, so without!" The world outside is created by the thoughts inside! If you want to change the outside, change the inside! Change the seeds, the thoughts you create! Your mind is like your blender—if you put oranges in it, they are pulverized and give you orange juice! If you want apple juice, start throwing in apples! And let the blender work to squeeze the apples! The law of karma simply means if you sow the seeds of oranges, never expect to reap apples! "Everything multiplies after its kind" is a law worthy of worshipping and reciting in daily life! Just as you select your shoes, clothes, and even car, be careful and conscious of the thoughts you select; they are the raw material out of which life is made! Your outside world is spun out of your very thoughts!

Make Every Day a Holy Day

Holy means "sacred, serene, and pure"! You can decide
to make every day holy; fill your mind with calming
thoughts! Think, speak, and do only with gratitude!
Gratitude cleanses your soul; it uplifts your spirit! It gives the giver
of gratitude a cleansing effect! It gives the receiver of gratitude a
humbling effect! There are two winners—the giver and the receiver!
Greet every day with gratitude in your heart! In the same way,
greet everybody whom you meet! Gratitude is love; gratitude is
care and compassion! It is the mother of all positive emotions!
It can neutralize negativity and heal with love! You are free from
fear when you are grateful! You are free from anger when you are
grateful! The effective prayer is always a prayer of gratitude!
When you are grateful, your ego is in check! A grateful mind is
ready to receive blessings! The holistic attitude is always feeling
gratitude! A heart filled with gratitude is the abode of God!
Yes! We can make every day a holy day—a day of peace,
tranquility, and serenity to find our true self! At the
end of every day, ask these two questions: *Who am I?*
and *What is my purpose on this beautiful planet?*

Message of Christmas

Love, joy, and kindness permeate Christmas! Jesus is the symbol of utmost sacrifice; he stood for love, peace, and harmony! He preached in the name of the Father, the Almighty! Jesus addressed God as the Father in heaven to make it easy for his apostles to follow! Basically, the biological father gives us three things! He gives the seed of life, refuge, and inheritance! The same way God alone gives us the gift of life, he gives us protection and refuge in times of crisis! But most of us forget the third gift of divine wealth! We are all heirs apparent to his divine inheritance! Understand the power of this third gift of wealth! You have the potential to grow your divinity, that spiritual power that is dormant like a coiled serpent! Once awakened, it can activate the all-knowing awareness! While visiting places of worship and devotion, remember the three gifts from almighty God to celebrate your life, in the name of Jesus Christ, by spreading love, peace, and heavenly harmony!

DESTINY

"Destiny has given us a book of rules, a bag of tools,
and a lump of clay," and we all must, and we all will,
make it a stumbling block or a stepping-stone!
Let us consciously look at every problem as an opportunity
in childish disguise! Fear is our eternal enemy, though an
impostor! We need to peel off this impostor's disguise!
The best way to deal with the fear is to do that which you are
afraid of and laugh it off! Fear is "fictitious events acting real"
(FEAR)! And have fear no more, and replace it with faith!
Look at every stumbling block as a stepping-stone; where
there is none, you create a new one! And leave it behind for
others to step on and overcome their own stumbling blocks!
Touch lives and make a difference in small ways, and your life
will be a paradise of endless joy! Who says one man cannot
make a difference? Make a commitment, and start now!

Be Positive Every Day

Things will happen—they do happen! But you can interpret
them in any way! Look for goodness in everyone! Look for
greatness hiding in adversity! "Hate the sin, but love the
sinner!" Love what you hate; bless that which hates you!
Appreciation is the twin sister of gratitude! Be grateful
for every breath you take! You never know: it could be the
last! If it is not, go down on your knees; say thanks!
Life is to love, and love is to give! Be a shoulder for
anyone to lean on! Think positive, talk positive, and act
positive! You will cultivate a grateful mental attitude!
Shed your old habits like a snake shedding its skin, learn new
ideas, and utter words that inspire! Fire your friends who are
negative thinkers! Surround yourself with positive vibrations!
Compliment your spouse without fail, and curb your tongue from
uttering hurt and shame! Love thyself, forgive thyself, and master
your emotions! You can discover your true self, loving kindness!
Always ask the question, *If not me, who?* Ask
the second question, *If not now, when?*

The Darkest Hour Is Just before the Dawn!

At one time or another, we all face a challenge or a dark
cloud threatening to blow us away! The world seems to
be crumbling around us rapidly, and the end seems to be
imminent and irreversible! All our efforts have become
barren, unproductive! And even God appears to have
forsaken us! These are the trying moments of life staring at
us, and we seem to have lost even our ability to think!
There are some of us seeing dark clouds over us now, ready to rain
on us, draining all our energy! All our friends and family remain
helplessly mute, and the very purpose of existence seems to be
at stake! When the Draculean fear has emptied our blood, and
courage seems to be slipping from our heart, and our head is reeling
like in a viral vertigo, we need to remind us, "This too shall pass!"
"The darkest hour is just before the dawn," we need to repeatedly
recite and remind ourselves so that we can muster all the strength
needed to stay calm and collected till the danger passes!
Life has a tendency to throw a curveball at us when we least expect
it, as though to test our grit, and we shall take all those challenges
head-on! We are sprouted in fire; we can handle any heat!

If I Could Go Back in Time ...

I am almost three-quarters of a century old! If I could go back in time fifty years, there is one thing I definitely would want to do: gain membership to a gym and go there religiously, at least five days a week—two days for weights and three days for aerobics, such as swift walking! Regular exercise is the foundation for living—healthy living, joyful and vibrational living! Regular physical activity invigorates the body; it promotes mental clarity, erases stress! It helps one sleep better, ensures proper digestion—the essential ingredients of a super immune system! An excellent immune system is an insurance policy against the invaders—bacteria and deadly diseases! The earlier you develop the habit of regular exercise, the more you can prevent lifestyle diseases such as diabetes, high blood pressure, high cholesterol, even cancer! If you are exercising, my hearty congrats! I have been a member of a gym for seven years now—the best decision I've made in my life for myself! I wish I'd made it in my younger days, but I did not! If you are thinking, *I do not have the time,* you are telling me it is not your priority! Believe me, find time; make it a priority for your health! You will be glad you did!

How Life Becomes a Self-Fulfilling Prophecy

Whenever you think of something constantly, it gets rooted in your subconscious mind! That sleeping giant with universal tentacles can convert your dreams into real experiences! Whenever you mix any desires with emotion, they will be picked up by the subconscious mind! And it will act on them, with all its invisible might, producing material equivalents of those desires! Words uttered with negative emotions produce a negative power known as a *destructive curse*! And words mixed with positive emotions can produce a boon, granting one's deepest desires! Our subconscious mind is the subjective mind! It is the obedient servant of the thinking mind! "What I have feared has fallen upon me," declares the New Testament, showing the power of fear! The subjective mind transcends time and space, with far- and wide-reaching spiritual tentacles! It is the seat of emotions and paranormal powers! It is the creative process in the mind of humans! Your subconscious listens to your inner desires day and night, as it never sleeps like the objective mind! This is the powerful ally of your thinking mind! Direct its power wisely to reap your destiny!

The Miracle of Hard Work

All your shortcomings can be overcome! It only takes hard work—passionate work—without worrying about the reward! You think you are not smart enough? Hard work can rectify that shortfall! You do not have a college degree? Hard work can cure that shortcoming too! You think you cannot study continuously for five years and defend your thesis to get your PhD? When you work for a year, you put in two thousand hours, and in five years, you work ten thousand human hours; it is equivalent to the study time of a PhD student. When you pour your heart into whatever work you do, your passion will induce your proficiency! A master craftsman can demand any wages he chooses! There is definitely a miracle in working hard! It will embolden you to accomplish more! Everyone in the office will start noticing you, and without your realizing it, you will become a star! Work hard, enjoy every moment, and never complain about the reward received! Divine justice will make sure that you are paid every penny with compound interest! How do I know for sure? I worked hard all my life and have been the recipient of multiple compound interests!

Chasing Love

Chasing love is like chasing a rainbow! We need to understand
the feeling of love! Love is like the right-of-way in our
driving; it is always to be given, never to be taken!
So is love—always give your love to one and all. Love
is the awareness that the spirit alone is flowing!
Start with loving you, understanding you! Then
love your neighbor as the Bible commands!
Chasing love is an exercise in futility, wasting time!
Many times, love comes in disguise, multiform! Love
is certainly respect, understanding, and care! It is
kindness, compassion, and a spiritual affinity!
Stop chasing love; start distributing love to all! You are
the inexhaustible well of love; give more! Unconditional
love is the true alpha and omega! It is perennial,
eternal, and never demanding of a thing!
Love others for what they are, rich or poor, young or old, black or
white or even colorless! Life is to love; love is to give. The more
you give, the more you get. It is the supreme universal law.

How to Change Your Past

Erase your past with a magic wand—it will not bother you anymore! We all like to lick our old wounds and relish the unconscious taste of them! In the process, we blame others for the wounds! This is how we carry excess baggage! Shed that burden once and for all! Getting freedom from the past is nirvana; free yourself, and move forward in life! Begin with sowing the seeds of change! Think of new ideas, new thoughts, and new words! Read new books, make new friends, and commit to change! Yes, you can do it! Yes, you alone can do it! Every snake sheds its old skin; so must we! Old habits are old and useless ways of living! Doing this can redeem your lust for life, passion, and vigor! Slowly but surely, transformation will happen! You are the master of your universe, the champion of change! Start doing it right now! Ask yourself, *If not me, who? If not now, when?*

THE ZEN SECRET

Before nirvana, chopping the wood and carrying water;
After nirvana, chopping the wood and carrying water,
What did then change?
Your attitude! Attitude is the predictor of success!
It is the *how* of life! Attitude is how you look at life!
Attitude is how you treat your wife or husband!
Attitude is how you treat your boss!
Attitude is how you treat your colleagues!
Attitude is how you treat a stranger!
Attitude is how you treat a homeless person!
Attitude is how you confront a challenge!
Attitude is how you solve a problem!
Attitude is how you live your life!
No wonder attitude dictates your altitude in life!

BORN TO WIN

You were born to win!
You were born to succeed!
You were born to make a difference!
The seeds of greatness have already been sown!
Nurture them with hope and gratitude!
You were made in the image and likeness
of the towering invisible creator!
You are not a bag of chemicals!
You are not made up of only bones and cells!
You were not born to be a crawling worm, existing
to eat, sleep, and freely reproduce!
The Creator intended you to be his heir apparent—
To distribute his glory and limitless compassion!
You were born to win! You were born to succeed!
You were born to make a difference!

Setting Goals or Making New Year's Resolutions?

Making a New Year's resolution is good; setting a goal is better! Resolutions are temporary, but goals are enduring! Incorporate your New Year's resolution into your goal setting! Goals are your guideposts in personal accomplishments! They give you a sense of purpose and a sense of urgency! Goals are the pillars of your personal growth! They are your taskmasters, and they keep you on track! Goals are your blueprints for success! They motivate you! They harness your subconscious mind! The daily ritual of reading your goals aloud impresses them upon your sleeping subconscious mind! Once you impress your desires upon the template of the subconscious, it will run with it! Using its spiritual tentacles, spread far and wide, it will help you achieve your goals, no matter what they are! Trust your subconscious with your goals! Recite them at dawn and dusk and midday! Back up your goals with enduring hard work and passion for your goals! Yes, you will definitely bag your goals! Start setting your goals today! Nurture them with passion and persistence along with hard work! You, too, can join the league of high achievers!

What Is Adversity?

Adversity is the university of higher learning!
It is chartered by real life itself!
It can teach lessons nobody can teach you!
It was my school of forced choice (forty-six years ago)!
It contains the seeds of lasting change!
It forces a paradigm shift in the student!
Adversity is the father of every achievement!
Adversity is progress in disguise!
Embrace adversity with a smile of hope!
You, too, will go places you never imagined!

TALKING FROM THE HEART

Start talking from the heart!
It is an art anybody can practice!
It will uplift and inspire others!
Your words will be calming and consoling!
Your tendency to judge will dissipate!
You will learn to harness your ego!
You will start touching many lives!
Your life will become more fulfilling!
And your purpose will dawn on the horizon!
And above all, you will become that person
Who you always wanted to be!

THE PRESENT MOMENT!

Life hides only in the presiding present moment!
Living in the present is the only true way of living!
The experience is real and invigorating!
Spending time dwelling on the past is a waste!
Dreaming about a faraway future is only futile!
Learn to experience in vivid details the present,
The true playground of eternal awareness!
The pain of the bygone past and the fear of the
future will no longer haunt you day and night!
Focus on the present, sharpen your senses, and live
like a monk, engaged only in the present!

Is your body a shadow of your mind?

There appears to be a direct connection!
The day you are in a good mood, your productivity increases!
The day something bothers you, your physical
body replicates the same feeling.
"As above, so below" is an ancient truth!
When you are not at ease in the mind, disease sets in!
All diseases start in the mind, and the body expresses them!
A clean mind is a prerequisite for a healthy body!
Entertain only healthy thoughts; your cells
and tissues will simply follow them!
Regular exercise is a panacea for a clean mind and a healthy body!

Why are thoughts powerful tools?

Every thought is a chip from the spirit!
The spirit is nothing but concentrated energy!
When you direct the concentrated energy toward
any goal, the goal becomes a reality!
Focus your thoughts on any goal, without any distractions; you
will achieve it! After all, matter is nothing but condensed energy!
Start focusing, and wonders will happen in your life!

Are you afraid of change?

Change is the essential fabric of life.
Change is the function of time; there are
uncertainties hidden in every change.
We must welcome change with open arms.
We must embrace change with all our heart!
We all learn new things with change.
Every change is a learning experience! Change
is the tool of empowerment!

Are rejections real?

Most of the rejections we feel are unreal;
They are the products of our own imagination!
You are jumping to a conclusion
Without any evidence to back it up!
Human behavior is very strange and inexplicable.
And people are not rejecting you;
They are telling you that your timing is bad
And to feel free to come back with a positive attitude!

Managing Emotions

Managing emotions is a pivotal act in daily living!
Understanding emotion is key to its management.
Every emotion is a psychophysical phenomenon
Caused by intense thoughts expressed in the body.
Once you are able to manage your thoughts,
You can learn to manage all your emotions.
Positive thoughts like love, compassion, and gratitude
Empower all parts of one's body and layers of one's mind.
They promote overall well-being and the immune system,
Whereas outbursts of negative emotions, like fear and anger,
Can play havoc on and weaken the immune system.
The role of emotions in our body and mind
Is critical knowledge we cannot afford to lack!

Power of Spirit!

Powered by the indomitable spirit,
You can soar like an eagle! You can roar like a ferocious lion!
You can land on the moon like Armstrong!
You can excel in any craft you choose!
You are the architect of your destiny!
You are the author of your book of life!
Yes! You can do it—only if you choose!

THIS ONE HABIT !

Happiness is a habit,
Like brushing your teeth!
Happiness can be cultivated on a daily basis!
Happiness is not about what you have!
Happiness is about what you are!
Happiness and unhappiness
Both exist in the field of time!
Thus, if you are happy, you are bound to be unhappy!
Understanding this truth will free you from chasing happiness!
The amount of happiness you derive in this
world is directly proportionate to the amount of
happiness you are willing to give others!

WHAT IS ~~A~~ LOVE?

Love is the art of knowing that the spirit alone is flowing!
Love others for who they are, not for what they have!
Love is like the right-of-way—always to be given, never to be taken.
Love what you hate; bless what hates you!
Love must always be unconditional; it has magical power!
Love yourself first; then love thy neighbor!
When you live to love, you will love to live!

The Power of Desire

Desire is the daughter of the spirit!
It can drive you crazy and nuts!
It is the alpha and omega of all creativity!
It is the secret of all human accomplishments!
It opens the doors of unlimited possibilities!
It is the gatekeeper of dreams!
It is a gift from God!
Whip up your desire, and unlock possibilities.

THE ONLY ATTITUDE!

Gratitude must be the only attitude in life!
Gratitude helps you be in the present moment!
Gratitude is a magic wand to erase negativity!
Gratitude is the ultimate in appreciation!
Gratitude helps you cultivate humility!
Gratitude is the soul's sincerest prayer!
Gratitude is the mother of all positive emotions!

The Ultimate Secret in Life

The ultimate secret in life is your power! You can use it in any way you want, and you do, but many times without realizing your power! You have the power to think; use discretion! Thoughts are things in the making, like acorns hiding in their wombs towering oak trees! The Taj Mahal was in the thoughts of the great Shilpi, who, upon the order from Shah Jahan, created it! You and I are the creators of all the things we have, though we seldom realize that we are the creators! Awake from this hallucination that others are the creators, when we, thought by thought, create our destiny! How is happiness possible when you harbor hatred? How is abundance possible when you think of limitations? Remove hatred, love others, and happiness will appear! Abundance is possible when limitations disappear! The ultimate secret is that thoughts are magnets! They attract their own kind, joy or sorrow! Start changing the way you think; alter your thoughts, and your life will turn around in a full circle! Create a life of abundance and lasting happiness! Yes, you can do it! You have been doing it wrongly! You have the green signal to alter your thoughts! Think of possibilities, love, abundance, and happiness!

THE Universal Purchase Order!

Your thoughts are your purchase order! Whenever you think with intention, you are putting the universe on notice that you want those things right now, and the universe simply executes your order! When your order arrives, you are sometimes very unhappy, because you thought of something you did not want! You placed the order without realizing that the universe would simply execute your order verbatim! Your intention has indomitable power to bring that which you intended, and except you yourself, nobody in the world can change your order! And this truth you have to internalize every day! Therefore, it is imperative that you refine your thoughts and make sure your order is correctly worded! The universe has no free return policy like Amazon! Whatever you ordered, you have to keep it! This is the biggest problem you face on this planet—you think of things you do not want to happen, then complain that somebody is out to get you! You are the creator of your own destructive destiny!

How to Accumulate Grace, the Spiritual Capital

1. Start writing in your journal of gratitude!
2. Cultivate a culture of compassion!
3. Practice empathy—listening without judging!
4. Do simple acts of kindness!
5. Show more respect to your wife or husband!
6. Avoid gossip completely; it only hurts!
7. Stop reacting; start acting with restraint!
8. Every day, read a few inspiring lines—your spiritamins!
9. Cultivate positive thoughts; pour emotion into words!
10. Be childlike and not childish!

GRACE = SPIRITUAL GOODWILL?

What is grace in life? *Grace* comes from the Latin word *gratia*, meaning "favor." God's unmerited favor is available to one and all! I consider grace *spiritual goodwill*, conferred to all for meritorious living and good deeds! When a person renders selfless service to society, it is a meritorious deed, performed out of love! How does God's grace benefit our daily living? A tennis ball hits us, instead of a stone, with grace! Nobody can escape the fruits of his or her actions! Yet with divine grace, their impact can be reduced! Gratitude is the door to divine grace! And love, compassion, and kindness will add to the pool! Every day, we ought to accumulate divine grace, as it will be like an insurance policy, covering risk! And many of the miraculous events we witness could be explained as divine grace in action for us!

WHAT IS HOLDING YOU BACK?

What is holding you back? You want to get that job, that promotion! You want to buy a bigger house, a nice car! You want to find the soul mate for your life! You want to be very happy and joyful, after all! But the future is bleak, and no hope is in sight! You do not know whom to ask, what to do. When life seems to hit a mighty roadblock, stop looking for answers outside! Go inside; you are always what you think! Read self-help books, and cultivate inspiring thoughts! Seek the company of high achievers who can help! Start doing new things; join a gym or the Speakers Club! Stop the blame game! Start using new vocabulary; add words like *inspire, thank you,* and *positive*! Change your demeanor; always be willing to help! Start teaching; volunteer to do things at your office! These tools of change are catalysts for a shift! A shift in perspective, the ultimate paradigm shift, starts from where you are! Forget the shortcomings! Maybe you had a bad childhood or your father did not smile! Look at the beautiful lotus: it begins in dirty mud, but it soars toward the sun to partake of its beauty! So can you, by letting your thoughts that create soar! Yesterday ended with last night; do not shed tears!

TSA ALIGNMENT!

Start practicing TSA alignment! Life is nothing but transacting with the universe! No matter who you are and where you are going, you think (T), you speak (S), and you act (A)! An alignment of thought, speech, and action is vital! The beginning of conflict is a lack of alignment! Just as a car wobbles when its tires are not aligned, so does misalignment make us start wobbling spiritually inside, causing emotional turmoil and physical unrest! Mean what you say, and say only what you mean! Your body language is intrinsically transparent! Your thoughts are the blueprints of the words that manifest as actions in your daily life! TSA alignment not only stops the internal turmoil but also protects your immune system, warding off disease! It is the key to mental harmony and spiritual uplift! This practice can jump-start your spiritual journey!

How to Deal with Better Experience or Bitter Experience

We always get either better experience or bitter experience. One we want to cherish for the rest of our life; the other one we want to forget as soon as possible! Really, the bitter experiences are our greatest teachers! Every experience comes to teach us a lesson! Learn the lesson, and move on with your life! Life is the best school of learning for all of us! When you connect the dots of the last decade, you can map out various events and their impact! Do not dive into the past and relive a bitter experience! Draw a lesson from it, say thanks for the lesson, and move on!

The Best Income-Tax Advice

As an income-tax consultant, I give only one piece of advice, which is the best advice! What is that advice? My advice and philosophy is to pay more income tax; then, your income will go up, and still, you will keep a large chunk of your earnings! Is it absurd? It is the best advice you can give! Around last tax time, a young friend called me! He was so excited and said, "Sir, I did it this year!" About seven years before, he had come seeking tax advice! He had wanted to reduce his income-tax liability! I had spent a couple of hours with him and convinced him it was fallacious to think about reducing his taxes! I had advised him to set a goal to pay $250,000 in income tax; he had not told me so at the time, but he had thought I was really crazy! But the idea had gotten glued, and his fear of taxes had vanished! This year, his income went up beyond his wildest imagination! Your fear can sabotage your potential in every field! Negativity steals your dreams, destroys your purpose! Transcend your fears by constantly thinking, *I can!* and you will be amazed at what you can really accomplish!

WHAT IS EMPATHY?

What is *empathy*? Empathy is a willingness to listen without judging! Empathy is spiritual connectivity in action! Empathy is openness without personal reservation! Empathy is about caring for another individual! Empathy is an aspect of unconditional love! Empathy is the road to one's true self! Empathy is about giving one's time and attention to another! Empathy is about opening the door to intimate personal relationships! Empathy is the supreme act of kindness! Empathy is the foundation of personal and social welfare! Empathy helps give the receiver a way out of his or her situation! Empathy ignites a spark of resilience in the empathizer and the empathized-for! Empathy is an expression of one's gratitude toward another! Empathy helps heal one's fractured ego! Empathy is about stepping into the spiritual shoes of another individual! Empathy is the basis of any type of conflict's resolution! Empathy lays the foundation for a deeper relationship!

Seven Tips for Mind Management

1. Stop reacting to events, conditions, and people!
Start acting, and take charge of your thoughts!
2. Practice gratitude in all areas of life! When you start appreciating
events and people, new events will appear in your life!
3. Compliment at least five people before going to sleep every night!
If you cannot, compliment your spouse or children five times!
4. Cultivate a culture of compassion. Think about compassion,
speak about compassion, and do acts of compassion!
5. Stop judging others! You never know the other
person's exact situation. You might act worse than the
other person if you were in his or her situation! *Shoes*
6. When emotions run high, keep your mouth shut!
Opening your mouth will only add fuel to the fire!
7. Even when things go wrong (as they many times do), recite,
"This too shall pass," several times. If you do not manage your
mind, somebody else will mismanage it for you—remember that!

A Spiritual Companion

Gratitude is your spiritual companion! With gratitude alongside you, you are highly empowered! You can solve all problems! You can face every challenge, every tragedy on earth! Gratitude is a spiritual tranquilizer; it can numb any heartache! Why is gratitude such a powerful emotion? Because of its very source—gratitude is rooted in divinity, a source of invigorating power! Did you know that gratitude is a way to one's spiritual journey? It facilitates total surrender to the all-pervading, almighty God! Gratitude neutralizes the negativity in you; it inspires you as it equally empowers the receiver of your gratitude! Wherever there is hate, gratitude lights a candle of love! Wherever there is ego, gratitude introduces humility! Gratitude is a spiritual catalyst, a transformative power! It can bring positive changes in every person practicing it! Add an attitude of gratitude to every aspect of your life, and your life will flower into the paradise of peace and harmony!

The Secret of Staying Inspired throughout the Day

This is the secret I discovered thirty-five years ago! I did not want to fall into the doldrums of frustration! It takes more time and pain than you think to come out of them, and the best thing is to keep yourself inspired at all times! So I started sharing my good thoughts with everybody I met—the people at the bank, the laundry, and the workplace and my kids! Slowly, I began to enjoy sharing and caring, keeping my cool! I began to practice new thoughts, new words, and new expressions! When you start sharing inspiration with others as a noble act, people get a kick out of it, and you stay inspired! Read more books, learn key phrases, and share with others! There are only winners, no losers, in exchanging inspiration! *Life is to love, and love is to give, and inspiration is pure love; ~~your problem of inspiration solved, you uplift others too!~~*
~~After four decades, this has become my silent mission in life!~~

You stay inspired at all times when you inspire others. After practice nearly four decades, it has become my silent mission in life!

Your Mind A Powerhouse!

It is all in your mind! "If you think success, success has begun; if you think you can win, your battle is won! Whatever you need you can have, you'll find: it's all in the way you set your mind" (K. W. Ruggles). The mind is the powerhouse for humankind!

We all know this, yet we sparingly use the power of this mighty giant. The duality of the mind is seldom understood; it is sad! We have a conscious mind and a subconscious mind! The conscious mind is the thinking mind, the logical mind! You must control the subjective mind, the emotional mind! The logical mind is the mastermind, directing the sleeping mind! The subconscious mind is all the more powerful yet obedient! Any deep-rooted desire you have will be translated to matter in the creative incubator of the subconscious mind! Understanding the workings of your mind is half the battle! Applying the power to make it happen is the rest of the battle!

Should you cry?

Do you cry very often? Crying is good because it cleanses your soul, so to speak! When emotions run high, both positive and negative, people shed tears and feel good in their trembling heart! They have tears of sadness and tears of joy; both are good! Men do not cry enough to shake off their built-up emotions! Women are experts when it comes to managing emotions! When emotions run wild, they cry and cry until they feel good! This is what nature intended to handle human emotions! Men need to cry more; being emotional is always a strength! You can connect with others and their pent-up emotions! When you cry, you produce lots of tears, enough to give your eyes a healthy bath, and tears make your eyes really beautiful! Men and women must cry as part of managing emotions! Heat produces rain in nature; people produce cleansing tears! Tears give you a feeling of relief and encourage a return to normalcy! So keep crying when you have to; you will have beautiful eyes!

Two Rules for Marital Harmony

We are all striving to do everything to preserve our marriages!
Men are reading too much about women—their likes, dislikes!
Women are frantically looking for ways to know the male ego!
Yet half of marriages, it is said, end in marital tragedy! But if
they follow two simple rules, men can save their marriages and
reap the fruits of marital harmony, experiencing marital bliss!
Man, swallow the male pride and uncontrollable ego of a maniac!
Understand the true nature of woman; she hates to have a loser!
Two rules are for daily repetition. Rule number one: Your wife
is always right! Rule number two: When in doubt, refer to rule
number one! Life is merely a sport. Do not take it seriously!

The Scorpion and the Frog

There lived on a small mango tree near a pond a scorpion, and in the pond, there was a friendly frog! They became friends, and every day, the scorpion would come down to chat with her friend, the friendly frog! One day, the scorpion expressed a strange desire to the frog: "My friend, it is my lifelong desire to swim in the pond. But, being a scorpion, I cannot swim, and I will drown." "No problem, my friend. I am a frog, always in the water. You can hop onto my back, and I will take you around." The scorpion was ecstatic, and the frog was happy to help. So they decided on a certain day and time for the adventure! The scorpion arrived on time, and the friendly frog was ready! The frog came to the shore so that the scorpion could hop onto him! When they set out on their adventure, the scorpion felt so good! The frog was very happy to have his friend in his habitat! However, halfway through the pond, the scorpion stung the frog! They both began to go down, and the frog asked the scorpion, "My friend, what happened? Why did you sting me, your friend?" The scorpion was sad and said, sobbing, "I am sorry, my friend! It is in my nature to sting, and I could not help it." Very true!

You ARE WHAT YOU THINK!

You are what you think! You and I are fully engaged in thought during our waking hours! The mind is the congregation of your thoughts; it is like a huge eagle's nest! When you stop the prattling of the mind, you do what is called *yoga*! *Meditation* is the gathering of your thought energy in a central place! If you think about liquor all day, you could end up in a bar! If you think about God all day, you could end up in a temple. Your thoughts are disturbances caused by your sense organs, and they are the messengers of the brain, the operational center! When thoughts run wild, they build a forest of confusion in us! When we cultivate thoughts consciously, we create a garden! Daily routine and rituals help us create useful thoughts! The alternative is chaos, lack of harmony, and utter confusion! The quality of our thoughts determines our quality of life! Discriminative thinking is the key to fostering a harmonious life! All religious rituals are geared to generate quality thoughts, which can transform into quality speech and quality action!

The Physiology and Psychology of Anger

We see anger as we witness wind or a hurricane moving fast! The formation of anger, however, we seldom get to see or witness! The *Bhagavad Gita*, the Hindu holy book, narrates anger stage by stage as it progresses in a human being! It says that when a man has an intense desire for some object, he constantly dwells on it without taking his inner eyes off it! Slowly, he develops an attachment, a mental process of intimacy! He really wants to possess and enjoy the object of his desire! When something or somebody becomes an obstacle to doing that, he becomes very angry; his outburst of anger is limitless! Anger traps him in a state of delusion when he loses his memory! With memory loss, his intellect takes a small vacation! The intellect is seated in the memory, and memory loss is deadly; with memory loss, he falls to the level of a beast, losing discrimination! The formation and natural evolution of anger is in the mind, and it expresses itself as a violent outburst in the physical body! Once you understand the evolutionary process of anger, you can take measures to manage it before it is too late! You can block the intense desire, the attachment, and its mental intimacy to free yourself from the ravages of anger!

One Day, a Jackfruit Fell, and a Rabbit Died ...

One day, a jackfruit fell, and a rabbit died! One day, you failed! One day, you made a mistake and failed the test of a lifetime! *One day* was a very bad day; you met with an accident! One day, you yelled at your significant other, and you cried! One day, the mahout got mad at the elephant; the elephant ran! One day, your teacher said, "You are dumb—no future for you!" One day, your boss got mad at you, and you got fired! One day, your father died, and your life filled with emptiness! These are "one day" events in life; they happen to all of us! You should not look at them as a pattern for your life! They are accidents, tragedies, or once-in-a-lifetime events! Do not shed tears and think your life is over and done with! Tomorrow, a jackfruit will not fall, and the rabbit will not be there to die! You will not make a mistake, and you will pass with flying colors! All that you have to do is try again without nagging doubts! Remain grateful, and learn from mistakes; it is not the end of the world!

The Best Way to Learn Is to Teach

Teachers are good students, attentive and studious! They show their passion for the subject under study! We can learn from the attitude and approach of teachers! The best way to learn is to teach, though it appears paradoxical! You do not have to look for a school or a college in order to teach! You can form a study circle at work or in the community; take a lead role to organize and coordinate the event! Teaching is an art; so is learning! You can learn to teach! Teaching is a noble act of sharing one's knowledge; what one knows about what subject is irrelevant! Volunteer to teach at a Sunday school; see the difference! Teachers have one thing in common—they adore repetition! Repetition is part of teaching. The more you share, the more you will know about anything! As you share with others, pay attention! With passion and attention, you can learn about anything!

How to Create Awareness of Everything

We always talk about awareness! It is the essence of life! Most of us, me included, sleepwalk through life—dozing! Thoughts happen; they come and go at the speed of light! Eventually, we realize what we are doing, but by then, the damage is already done! To experience life, we need acute attention, known as *sraddha*, the Sanskrit word for "awareness, attention, ultimate focus"! Awareness is the key to thought management and self-discipline! What you do not manage will mismanage you! Unfortunately, it is said that "the devil is in the details"; pay attention to details! Can you look intensely at something? Make it a practice to do so! Look at a beautiful flower, a butterfly, or even your baby! Pay close attention to details; then, you are really in meditation! You are already doing it when you really get lost in thought! Expanding the horizon of awareness in everything you do will make you enjoy life like never before—as an addiction! This passion is the key to joy and everlasting success in life!

Respect Is the First Rule of Engagement

Respect yourself, and start respecting others! Respect must be the first rule of engagement for all! Respect your spouse and children for who they are, not what they have or what they do for you personally! Respecting others is the foundation of your self-esteem! It defines who you are, not others to whom you show respect! Respect is reverence, appreciation, high esteem and love, the fundamental behavior for all, no matter who you are! Respect is the pillar of personal integrity and wholesomeness, the right way to treat others no matter what they have! You must teach your children to respect you as their parent as well as their teachers, their friends and their friends' parents, and everyone they meet in life! When you respect everything created, the respect goes to the creator—the architect of the universe who gave you the gift of life! Respect everyone as though he or she is your mother or father! Cultivate a culture of utmost reverence to celebrate your life!

STRANGERS IN LIFE?..

Are there strangers in life? There are no strangers except in your mind! There are people whom you do not know yet! But understand in your gut that they are humans, your own kith and kin connected always by the spirit! Once you know who you are, you have no strangers! Your name does not define who you are; it is for identification! Others may not know you until you connect with them! You can connect with anyone if your intentions are pure! If you have good intentions, you will never have strangers—only friends in the making, companions in this journey of life! Your wife of today or husband of today you did not know until you met, talked, and found each other to be soul mates! You are the universe! You hold the power to make friends! Appreciate everyone regardless of look, gender, or demeanor! Send your blessings to one and all; they will feel your love! Kinship is the truth, friendship is an experience, and love is immortal!

Yesterday Ended with Last Night

Yesterday ended with last night! Why are you still living there? You waste half your life thinking about yesterday's failures, yesterday's pain, yesterday's guilt, and yesterday's problems! The sun went down; still, you are staring at the dark horizon! It is over, and you had terrible pain; you are reliving it again! Every experience comes to teach you a lesson; learn the lesson! Move on without reenacting the drama of a painful ordeal! It is a sheer waste of energy and loss of life, as time is life! Living in the present is life! It empowers, uplifts, and energizes! It creates new opportunities, new experiences, and inner joy! Always remind yourself that yesterday ended with last night! It is time to move on and seek new experience in life! Life is a limited time; no one ever has the luxury of eternity! Employ every moment of life in a worthwhile endeavor! The past is pain, the future is fear, and the present is life and a source of joy! Understand this truth that yesterday ended with last night!

How to Overcome Your Shortcomings

Everything in this world is created twice—first in thought and second in the material world as a touchable, seeable reality! Rather than talking about your shortcoming in public, make up your mind to take action and cure it for yourself! Write down your one shortcoming, and lay out your plan! Step by step, visualize the details of your action plan! Many times, your shortcoming is a figment of your imagination! Others do not see it the way you do; only you are over-conscious! Albert Einstein's fifth-grade teacher thought he was dumb, yet he became probably the most intelligent mortal who has ever lived! Michael Jordan was rejected from a school basketball team, yet he broke records upon records and became the best in the game! Abraham Lincoln failed in everything he touched, yet he became one of the greatest American presidents in history! Thomas Alva Edison was a mere newspaper boy and failed a thousand times before he invented the modern-day light bulb! It is not who you are now that really matters! Focus on the future—where you want to be a year, two years, and five years from now! Begin with the end in sight; visualize the way you want to be! Stop displaying your shortcoming and looking for sympathy!

Stress Management with Emotional Wisdom

Managing stress is one of the challenges of modern living! Even a two-year-old child seems to have stress these days! Maybe it is the parents' stress; the child is inheriting it, so to speak! We have created a stressful society looking for calmness! Stress is mismanaged thought energy running amok without a direction, causing physical and emotional turmoil. When left unchecked, it can lead to high blood pressure and a host of lifestyle ailments such as hypertension and diabetes! Watching your thoughts is one way to understand thought! Thought observation is key to managing thought energy! Emotional wisdom teaches you to watch your emotions and prevent emotions like anger and fear from getting out of control! Regular physical exercise and meditation can effectively help you manage emotions, as awareness of the problem is the key! A daily regimen and meaningful rituals such as meditation can help you manage your stress beyond your imagination! When emotional knowledge is validated by one's life experience, emotional wisdom is born, bringing certain disciplines in life! These daily disciplines and awareness of who you are will help reduce your stress level and make you live a stress-free life!

The Panacea for Unhappiness

Unhappiness sets in when you are not happy and have nothing going on, with the same old stuff stealing your energy and enthusiasm! You are always drained of energy; there is no hope in sight! At home or work, you are just tired, cannot even sleep! If you are happy, you are bound to be unhappy without a doubt, as both happiness and unhappiness exist in the field of time! We are all like children, as they get bored with the same toy, and adults get tired of the same thing again and again! The panacea for unhappiness is an attitude of gratitude! It embraces everything with a sense of appreciation! Gratitude is a positive emotion that neutralizes negativity! There can be no unhappiness without negativity in the mind! When you are grateful, you forget and forgive; stay calm! Even when there are challenges, transcend them with a smile! Gratitude is the mother of all positive emotions; it uplifts! And your mind will not be infested with a negative attitude! A daily drill of gratitude makes your positive emotions very strong! You become the master of your own mind, always in control! Gratitude must be the only attitude in life! It empowers you! Your unhappy days will be a thing of the past with gratitude!

An Anchor Thought to Anchor Your Mind

An anchor firmly holds a ship so that it will not drift into the sea even when a strong wind is blowing! It is in the innate nature of your mind to drift when left unattended too! If you have a strong thought, use it as an anchor thought! This is what mantras are for—as anchors to arrest your mind! Every mantra is indeed a spiritually charged chain of words! You can use any strong and inspiring word as an anchor if you do not have a mantra to anchor your restless mind! When you are not doing anything, or you are driving, you can use the anchor thought to bind your mind to prevent it from drifting away into the sea of confusion! And this will preserve your precious mental energy for the better! Start using this very effective mind-management tool, and you will soon find yourself with a well-rested mind! An unruly mind is worse than a devil playing havoc with you! And your job is to expel this devil from your mind forever!

THIS WORLD IS AN ECHO!

The world is an echo! Once, a ten-year-old boy got mad at his loving mother because she did not allow him to go out to play! He was so mad at her he ran up the hill behind their home and shouted at the top of his voice, "I haaaaate you!" The echo, "I haaaaate you!" came back so loud and clear the little boy got scared and ran back to his mother. Trembling, he said, "Mom, there is a spirit behind the hill. He shouted, 'I haaaaate you!' I am scared, Mom!" said he. The loving mom understood what had happened and told her son, "You go back there and shout back, 'I looooove you!'" The young lad ran back to the hill and shouted, "I looooove you!" The echo came back, "I looooove you!" The boy was happy! This world is an echo, giving back to you what you release! You start loving one and all, and love will come back to you! If you hate everybody, hate will come back to haunt you! The truth is that what you have sown, you have to reap, for sure!

You do not have to Suffer!

Are you in pain? If you believe in Gautama Buddha, you know pain is inevitable! But are you suffering? Suffering is optional, says the enlightened one! Mental anguish is pain! Anxiety is pain! So is agony or fear! To prevent suffering, you need to understand pain! There is a cause-and-effect relationship in the universe! Every effect has a cause! The effect is the aftermath or symptom! Many times, we end up treating the symptom or the effect! We can mask the symptom by treating it, but the cause still remains! When you dig deep into the cause of mental agony, you can locate the source of the pain, a mental disturbance! Those disturbances many times are faulty perceptions starting from wrong data and fallacious conclusions! Anytime you feel a disturbance, pause; look at its cause! And see, if you identify the cause, you can eliminate the cause! Many pains are self-inflicted and imaginary, not real! Understanding the cause of the pain prevents suffering!

Be alert with every pain, shun the victim mentality, and be brave! And dig deeper for the cause; give up bias and judgment! The intensity of the pain gets reduced with close examination! And suffering is prevented because you know the cause!

How to Handle Fear of Failure

Fear of failure is an indomitable power holding us back! The more you think about fear, the more you become frozen, unable to think, unable to move forward and do anything! Many times, the fear is so paralyzing that you become a stone! Fear of failure haunts you because your mind is fixated! You must release the mind from this state of fixation to find flexibility! You can bring a freshness to the mind by reading about failures, stories of Thomas Edison, Abraham Lincoln, or Gandhi! When you know those, you know confidence replaces fear! Alter your thoughts; bring fresh, vibrating thoughts to mind! The mind is like a very hungry dog—it needs new bones to chew on! Keep deliberately feeding fresh thoughts to the mind now! The dog will keep chewing old bones until it gets new ones; we have a tendency to cling to the past like a slave! You need to find new pathways for the mind, new thoughts! This is the secret of handling fear of failure or any fear!

A Spiritual Shock Absorber?

Why do you need emotional wisdom? "Pain is inevitable. Suffering is optional," said Gautama Buddha! We all need emotional wisdom to reduce suffering! Life throws at us different challenges, many times curveballs that are seemingly impossible to handle, even taking the breath out of us! It is absolutely a fact that nothing is happening outside of you, as the whole process of perception is an internal one! Your different faculties of mind process all the information! Preparing the mind to effectively process the information is key! Emotional wisdom sharpens your tools of perception every day! Life will continue to throw challenges at you, but you are ready! Do you know how to handle the death of a dear one? Emotional wisdom prepares you for that shocking event! Do you know how to handle losing your job for no reason? Emotional wisdom prepares you to handle the shock effectively!

Emotional wisdom is nothing but a spiritual shock absorber, swallowing daily shocks with the least amount of damage to you!

Are you bored with life?

Are you bored with life? We all get bored with something when it becomes stale—stale food, stale clothes, stale friends, and even a stale marriage! When perception becomes monotonous and acutely biased, boredom sets in like an infection attacking the human body! Sharpening your perception is the best solution for boredom! Cultivating curiosity like a child can enhance your perception! Sitting with your eyes closed for a few minutes induces perception! With sharpened perception, your faculties become wide-awake! Physical exercise is another way to activate your body and mind! It can not only enhance your brain but also balance your emotions! When your body and mind are activated, you sleep better! And the monotony and boredom will begin to depart forever!

Giving is Receiving!

Giving is receiving! When you give, you are indeed receiving—in
spirit! You are part of the universe! So is the humble receiver!
In the universal family of the spirit, giver and receiver are one!
The appearance of duality is a mirage, just a different illusion!
Giving always stimulates the universe to reward the giver! "It
is in giving that we are receiving" is the ultimate universal law!
It is a privilege to give—an opportunity to help another soul!
Do not make the receiver feel obliged to the act of receiving!
Life is a journey from the cradle to the graveyard for all of us!
Ownership is a myth! It can only massage your bulging ego!
Grab every opportunity to give, removing the mask of the giver!
Remain grateful for the opportunity to extend a helping hand!

ONE PERSON ARMY 2.

You are a one-person army! Who says one person cannot make a difference? Yes, you can! Touch one life at a time with simple acts of kindness in your family, in your community, and even in the workplace! God is everywhere, and he needs you to help in his *HCS* mission! Life is a pilgrimage to selfless service with unwavering devotion! "When the student is ready, the teacher will appear"— very true! When you are ready, the opportunities will begin to appear! Make up your mind to lead your one-person army to do good! Life is too short; make it fun for you and others around you! Talk less; listen more! Make your presence felt by doing only! Laziness and inertia decorate the fools who find excuses! Wise ones constantly try to make a difference in others!

You ARE Unique!

Celebrate your uniqueness! You are one of a kind! There is no one just like you! You might falter and fall at times, yet you can muster the courage to get up and go and reach your ultimate goal with ease! It is your uniqueness that you should worship; it can do wonders! You do not need to be taller or more handsome or even smarter! The creator endowed you with a power ready to expand! Know what you want, and take action and be ready to fail! People who did not fail never got up from their seat! If you have any doubt about your uniqueness, ask your mother! She is the only person who can talk to you with maternal love! You do not have to emulate another or seek a role model! You are self-sufficient: uniquely placed and wired for success! You were born to win! You were born to succeed! You are unique! The world is waiting; the universe is ready to help you! Celebrate your uniqueness, and plunge into action with no hesitation! Your mother cannot tell you a lie, as she is your very own!

ARE WORRIES REAL ?.

What are your worries? Worries are your imaginary devils,
haunting you! Many times, they are borrowed worries, borrowed
from others! You talk to a friend who worries about something,
and thinking about the worry, your imagination magnifies it!
As Dale Carnegie put it, "Ninety-nine percent of your worries
are unfounded," and the one percent is out of your control!
So why worry about that which is beyond your control? Do
not dwell on your worries, as they are real invitations! Every
thought you think is an invitation for its appearance! So think
about only things that you want to see in your life! "What I
have feared has fallen upon me" is true about worries! Stay
focused on things you want, and worries will flee forever!

Show RESTRAINT!

Can you smile when your wife is yelling at you? I hope you both
then stop yelling at each other! The preceding question is your
litmus test for if you are acting instead of reacting! When you *act*,
you are in control; you are the master! When you *react*, you are a
slave, a floor mat for others! Training yourself to act in any situation
is the first lesson in emotional wisdom! Others can yell at you; you
smile! Your smile does not say you are insensitive or stonyhearted;
it shows you understand and you will take action to correct yourself
after yelling at another person, no matter who it is! No way you
can say sorry and cure the emotional scar! An ounce of prevention
is more effective than a ton of cure! It preserves self-respect and
respect for loved ones! The fortress of emotional freedom is the
capacity to act even in trying situations, navigating your mind
with ease! Write down two situations you will not react to in a day!
Keeping the score of every day's action, you will master the art!
Day by day, in every situation, you show empathy by acting! Any
fool can react and feel good about massaging the ego! But strong
is the one who chooses to act wisely in all situations! Do this, and
you, too, will join the company of masters who show restraint!

You Are The Problem!

You are the problem! Kindly examine this statement, and analyze it unbiased! We are the creators and solvers of all our problems! They exist mostly in our imagination—a faculty of our mind! Our mind is our apparatus of perception, a tool for transacting! Poor mind hygiene, no oil change and no regular tune-up, causes our mind to lose its capacity to run like a well-kept car! Do not wait until your house is on fire to look for ~~an~~ a fire extinguisher! Do not wait until you are stressed-out to look for a solution! Keep your mental faculties sharp with daily examination! Watch your thoughts; observe them with acute attention! Pay attention to anything and everything that comes to you! There are no big things, only small things making a big difference!

Act As Though _ _ _ _ _

Fake it till you make it! Act as though you are happy and successful; you will become that if you persist and never give up! The great Harvard professor and psychologist William James advocated the now-famous *as if principle*! He said to live the life of your dreams, at least in your imagination; that is a stepping-stone to the actualization of those dreams! The creative mind, which lies hidden in the deeper layers of the mind, does not know the difference between synthetic and actual! This subjective mind simply obeys your conscious thoughts; it does not argue or discriminate between good and bad! It is like a sponge; it absorbs everything you impress upon it! If you think you are dumb, it will make sure you are dumb! Hence, you have to be careful what you ask for. You can also use this trait of the subconscious to your benefit! Act as though you are wealthy; you will be sooner or later as you persistently follow that behavior pattern! Why do the poor become poorer even after winning a lottery? Because they think poor, and it manifests as a touchable reality! Whatever you want to achieve in life, act as though you have it; the subconscious will work hard to make it happen for you!

You are a Creator!

Are you a creator or a creature? We are always trying to be either creatures of circumstance or creators of circumstance, new and vibrant! If you are trying to conform and fit yourself where you are, there is nothing wrong with that, but you are just another creature! If you don't like what you see, create your own circumstance! Join the company of the shakers and movers of this planet; by doing this, not only are you taking the road less traveled, but you are also creating a new one where there was none! As James Allen put it, "Circumstance is merely a looking glass." It confirms what is going on in your inner world, for the world outside is a simple reflection of the world inside: "As above, so below!" Current thoughts are merely manifesting! Learn to create new circumstances; be a creator, not a creature crawling the surface of the earth, helpless and beaten down! You were created in the image and likeness of the creator! Realize this truth, and shake off your cloak of limitations!

ALIGN WITH THE Universe!

Are you the chosen one? It is a privilege to be part of this universe!
It is a blessing to be born as a human being! The universe consists
of everything seen and unseen, everything heard and unheard,
everything felt and unfelt! It includes everything smelled and
unsmelled, tasted and untasted! It is organic and inorganic;
it encompasses the whole of creation! You cannot fight this
indomitable energy; it can crush you! Yet you can ally with this
power, make it your spiritual partner! You are part of this universe,
the undefined, powerful royalty! You can accomplish anything
you want when you align with it! Knowing this truth is half
the battle; applying it is the other half! You are given the same
opportunity as the richest man living! You must know what you
want! Success is like a maiden; she wants the whole of you, your
unwavering commitment! Many people fall by the wayside when
they get discouraged! The universe wants you to pour out your
passion and emotion! Ask yourself this fundamental question:
*Am I fighting it, or am I allying with this powerful force and riding
the wave?* Grab this opportunity; align with the universe starting
now! You are the supreme creation, endowed with intelligence!

How to Tame Your Ego

We all need a certain amount of ego to keep us going! But when it raises its ugly head all the time, we need to tame it to be effective and in control! Allowing our ego to run amok is suicidal! One sign that your ego is out of control is you crave to judge everyone and find fault with others frequently! You judge other people to show that you are better than them—a classic need for the ego to survive and prosper every day! An attitude of "my way or the highway" is another sign that your ego is out of control and needs to be restrained! Using vulgar language and putting others down is yet another sign that your ego is getting out of control! Many times, a superego is the result of low self-esteem! One thinks acting superior will mask an inferiority complex; the paradox is that everyone else understands your problem, yet you keep going with your defeating ego massage! One solution for an uncontrolled ego is reminding yourself of your mortality! We are all here for a short visit; none is here forever! Second is cultivating humility, the attire of greatness, and emulating leaders like Gandhi and Mother Teresa! How do you stay charged all the time? A clean mind and a healthy body you must sport! And keep your enthusiasm at the highest level! When you do that, confidence replaces fear! Confidence is the lifeblood of staying charged! It is said that a charged magnet can lift ten times its weight! When it is demagnetized, it cannot lift even a feather! So it is with us, the human beings; when we are charged, we do greater things! And when we lose the charge, we are hopelessly ineffective! Surround yourself with friends who are upbeat and cheerful! Stay away from doubting Thomases and naysayers! Fire some of your friends if they demoralize you constantly; be active, and lead a purposeful life! Be a shoulder for others and always curious like a child; and let others interest you! Be a good listener and a go-to person in the community! Live as though it is your last day and explore as though you just arrived, and you will be charged like a magnetized steel rod!

The Art of Visualization!

Always begin with the end in sight! The master said, "Whatsoever ye shall pray and ask for, believe ye have received, ye shall receive!" This is a classic example of the effective use of visualization! You see the end result before your mind's eye when you begin! The subconscious can be activated in the present! It is like a sponge; it will absorb anything you impress upon it! The subconscious is a fertile soil, like a child's mind—innocent, naïve, and ready to act on your command, whether or not it's true! It is not the logical, arguing mind; it is the obeying mind, capable of translating all your dreams into reality! It does not know the difference between synthetic and actual! It is like a blender, which will blend the fruits in the jar you dropped! Visualization is the tool of transformation; use it with care! You can harness the power of the subconscious mind! Visualization is a spiritual prototype of your dreams! They manifest in a material form in its creative incubator!

Fear is Imaginary!

Are you trying to cut down an imaginary tree? This is what addressing your fears amounts to! Fear is a figment of one's imagination, nourished by repetition! Write down your fears one by one and their consequences! At the end of this, you will know they are fragile and fictitious! Every fear is a product of your imagination, acting very real, and it takes root in your subconscious mind over time! Whatever you impress upon your subjective mind is a belief! It is almost impossible to shake off an old belief! Can you cut down a tree that does not exist in the real world? So is trying to remove a fear that is imaginary, not real!

EVERY THOUGHT — AN INVITATION)

Think good, and good will always follow! Think good; the alternative is miserable meanness! Every thought is a seed of the thing to manifest! It is an invitation to the universe to supply you that thing! A powerful intention is the secret of every accomplishment! Do you want to be happy, successful, and productive? Or do you want to be mean, lazy, and a burden to society? It is your choice; you alone can choose your path! Others can help you, support you, and encourage you! Do you want to be around people who are miserable? Or do you love to be surrounded by a good and vibrant group? Your thought is a spiritual invitation to the universe! This, in fact, is the basis of the law of attraction!

Ugliness Is in the Eyes of the Looker

We are told that beauty is in the eyes of the beholder! But ugliness is equally in the eyes of the looker! Spiritually brighten your eyesight with a clear vision! Try to see the creator himself in the created pieces of beauty! Can you tell any mother her son is ugly or ignorant? Respect every mother like your own; make her proud! Never criticize any person; everyone has a role to play! That is the director's decision; respect almighty God! We are all here for a purpose! Focus on your purpose! Help others live their purpose!

Life is a simple mission—a mission to live and let others live their life their own way! It is never "my way or the highway"! Be compassionate to others! When you live for yourself, life is utterly miserable and mean! When you live for others, it is pure joy, with the creator's blessings! Remind yourself of mortality every day, every hour! Every breath is a gift; everybody is a borrowed body! and borrowed time!

has

My Biggest Blessing

My biggest blessing came as an impostor—a financial disaster at the young age of thirty-six! In today's dollars, it was a million dollars and change! My business venture went south, pulling me down with a growing family and a fully devoted wife! My world went upside down, making my head spin! I was trying to find answers like a dog trying to catch its own tail! *What went wrong? How would I come out of it? Could I?* I looked for answers hidden in the pages of ancient books and the wisdom shared by philosophers like Socrates! And I decided to stay away from cigarettes, drugs, and alcohol! I wanted to be a father for my three lovely, loving boys! I decided to bite the bullet, taking full responsibility without blaming anybody for my dismal failure in life! Without causing any commotion in my family, I worked—worked hard indeed—to get out of debt and succeed! In my spare time, I found refuge in very old inspirational books, like *As a Man Thinketh*, *Acres of Diamonds*, and the like! Without my knowledge, I began to change internally as my vocabulary filled with hopes and hopeful emotions! After four years of hard work and a positive mental attitude, I could see light at the end of the tunnel—a welcome relief!

Happiness Is a Habit! Cultivate It!

Like any habit, happiness can be cultivated! Staying pleasant regardless of what comes is an art you can master with practice; when you do, you will enjoy every moment of life on this planet! Look at the glass as half-full, not half-empty! Be optimistic about life; expect the best! External stimuli, however enchanting they may be, cannot bring permanent joy and happiness! Happiness is an attitude toward life; gratitude must be your only attitude, no matter what! Attitude is the attire of your character—nothing else! Remain grateful under all circumstances, as Saint Paul said! When faced with a grave situation, you must have the mantra "This too shall pass" to get you out of the situation! People who find joy in life are the ones who are hopeful! Expecting the best is the key to getting the best in life!

Your CLEAN up THOUGHTS!

Do you clean up your thoughts every day? We all clean our teeth every day as part of hygiene! Don't we need to clean up our thoughts too? As part of spiritual hygiene, we all need to do it! Now, we hide our thoughts; start opening up! When your thoughts are clean, they are healthy! They can uplift others and make a difference! Believe me, bad thoughts smell worse than an unclean body! They create incurable emotional disturbances! You do not need a brush and paste to clean them; you sit in one place and watch your thoughts! Let all thoughts come and go; simply watch them! Thought observation is the best form of hygiene! Thoughts are like thieves—simply stare at them, and they will flee! And an exercise will keep you healthy—let the whole world see your clean thoughts, and your own thoughts will thank you for that!

Are You Asking the Universe?

The New Testament says, "Ask and you shall receive"! But most of us are not receiving, and why? Because we are not asking the right way! How do you ask the universe the right way? Align your thoughts, speech, and actions always! They form your communication apparatus! Total harmony of thought, speech, and action is the right way and only way to ask the universe! Without it, your asking is shallow with no intensity, no bite! Your deep-rooted intention for what you seek is the key to effectively asking the universe! There is another smart way to ask the universe—whatever you want in life, start giving it, and it will come back to you multiplied, for sure! The law of reciprocity is at work! It is an inviolable law of the universe; follow it! Life is an echo! You get back that which you give! When you say, "I looooove you!" the echo "I looooove you!" will come back. When you say, "I haaaaate you!" the echo "I haaaaate you!" will come back. This is the simplest way of explaining karmic law! You know now how to ask for what you want! Practice using your tool of communication! The universe is very kind; you be kind to it as well! Love one another, and you will live a blissful life!

The Law of Reciprocity Revisited

Are you still yelling at your wife or husband? We talked about the aftermath of doing that! The law of reciprocity is always working for us! For peasants and presidents, it works the same way! The law of reciprocity says the universe reciprocates in kind, tit for tit, this for this—the same! If you respect someone, the universe will respect you too; multiplicity is its general rule! If you help a homeless man, you are virtually helping the universe! If you help your child do her work, you are helping the universe! If you kick a can in the street, the universe is there receiving the kick and will certainly reciprocate! Universal laws are inviolable; they are supreme! Understand this, and align with them to benefit! Everything, including you, is part of the universe! Understand this truth, and make it your ally! Allying with the universe, you are so powerful! Nobody can touch you! Nobody can defeat you! No matter what you want, it is just for the asking! "Ask and you shall receive" is a biblical proclamation!

THOUGHTS ARE SEEDS!

Why are thoughts things? "Thoughts are things," we hear all the time! Is it true? What makes these thoughts things? How can you capitalize on this theory? This is a question worth pondering to realize your dreams! Thoughts are nothing but chips of spiritual energy! The spirit is matter in its purest form, ready to convert! The universe is nothing but energy; we are told it cannot be created, nor can it be destroyed! Your mind is a thought percolator, always acting on the thoughts you submit like a food processor! Thoughts are the blueprints for germination! They sprout as matter in your creative incubator! Thus, your intense thoughts, holding on like leeches, will transform themselves into touchable matter! Thoughts are indeed the seeds of matter; trust that! Select those wisely, and you will translate your dreams!

The Truth about Anger

Why are people getting angry at you? The truth about anger is that people are angry at themselves for something, generally an act of commission or omission! Next time somebody gets angry at you, ignore it! And do not try to justify yourself; it does not matter! The angry person is a victim of his or her habit! The habit of getting angry accumulates over time! If you get angry at somebody, pause, reflect, and think! What is that thought bothering you enough to get angry? Anger is like a thief; when you stare, he will flee, so try this technique next time you are getting angry! I have another interesting technique I use: I tell others to give me a week to be angry! Rome was not built in a day; so is it with your anger habit! Start today, and in ninety days, you will overcome anger!

You Are the Universe!

You are the universe! Nothing happens outside! Your thoughts create the thoughts world! You are the prisoner of your thoughts, for sure! Knowing and internalizing this is the real battle! Are you a prisoner of your fearful thoughts? Are you a prisoner of your other negative thoughts? Can you alter them to thoughts of faith, gratitude, or love? Of course, you can choose faith, gratitude, or love! The farmer knows what he wants to sow today! If he wants barley, he only sows the seeds of barley! He knows that he cannot reap barley sowing wheat! Do you think even for a moment about what you want? You want to be happy, you think of unhappy events! You want to be wealthy, you condemn wealth! You are doing the opposite of what you want! Walking west, you cannot reach east! Your imagination is your asset; use it wisely! Think of things you want to realize in your life! Choose your thoughts; hold on to them; watch them germinate and grow into a full harvest!

How to Master Your Today

Yesterday ended with last night, and tomorrow never comes!
What are you left with? Only today! Focus on the present; reap
joy! Living in the present means only that! When you are in
the office, don't think of your wife! And don't think of your
office and work when you are with your wife and children!
Women are very good at compartmentalizing! They have greater
emotional wisdom than men! Your mind is plastic, teachable,
and coachable! Start altering your thoughts, changing behavior;
it is not that difficult to alter thoughts! Think new thoughts!
Read new books! Master new vocabulary; practice new deeds!
You are already on the right path! Just do it! As soon as you get
up in the morning, smile! You are lucky you are alive; many
people are not! Do not take life for granted; every breath is a
gift! Appreciate that; you are on the path of real change!

Why Are the Rich Getting Richer?

Rich people think of wealth all the time! They move with other rich people! They do not play the blame game! Their vocabulary is inspiring and positive! They waste no time in gossiping! They like to contribute to charities! They save and invest their savings! They focus on what they want in life! They have big dreams; they chase them always! They seldom complain about others! They praise wealth and handle it with respect! They are scared of wasting money! They live a modest life and save more! They cannot throw money away!

A Grateful Mental Attitude

Develop a grateful mental attitude—a GMA—and you will
overcome all your obstacles with ease! Gratitude is appreciation for
everything around you—people, animate and inanimate objects!
Gratitude is an expression of respect, love, and care! An attitude of
gratitude is the ultimate winner! It can erase negativity, hatred, and
one's own ego! GMA is a panacea for all human ills, all problems!
GMA is a spiritual cleanser; it is a spiritual catalyst! It can penetrate
even rocklike hearts! Gratitude opens the pathway to spirituality!
It frees the mind from fear, anger, and human greed! Practice
GMA! It can elevate you to become a better person—your need to
appease your ego departs very slowly! And stimulate every kind of
positive vibration to take you to the next level of spiritual uplift!

ARE YOU WALKING WEST?

Are you walking west? There was a man who lived in Elmhurst, twenty miles directly west of Chicago, Illinois! He wanted to go to Chicago, situated east of Elmhurst! Every day, he set out of his home toward Wheaton—Wheaton is a town ten miles west of Elmhurst—and he complained that he did not reach Chicago! You want to be wealthy, and you criticize wealth! You want to be healthy, and you think of sickness! You want to be successful, yet you court failures! You want to be happy, and think unhappy thoughts! Are you not like the man who walked toward Wheaton and complained that he never reached Chicago? We need to walk in the direction of our dreams! We need to fall in love with our life goals! Cultivate a passion—a kind of spiritual infatuation! It is only a matter of time; you will reach your goals! Admire and adore wealth in your waking and sleeping hours! Think healthy; court only health-inducing thoughts! You will be successful and fall in love with success! And finally, you will reach Chicago walking east!

Remember Two Things!
Forget Two Things!

One day, little Johny came home crying after attending Sunday school! His loving mother knew something was wrong! "My son, what happened at the school?" she asked. Little Johny wiped his tears and said to his mom, "I do not want to die, Mom. Then, I will lose you!" "Who said you have to die?" asked his loving mom! "Teacher said I have to die to reach heaven," said Johny. Mother could see the anguish in his little eyes, and she said, "You will be happy forever. Listen to me: you remember two things and forget two things, and you will always be happier than being in heaven!" Little Johny's eyes lit up, and he asked his mom, "Tell me two things I must remember every day!" "Remember God, and remember your parents," said Mom. "Thanks, Mom. What two things must I forget?" "Johny, forget all the good things you do for others! And forget all the bad things others have done to you!" The little child embraced his mom with teary eyes! Mother smiled, and both got lost in their embrace!

How to Ignite a Fire in Your Belly

A fire in your belly is a must for a sales professional! It is like fuel to an engine; it helps you stay focused! Goal-setting rituals help ignite a fire in the belly! Practicing visualization ensures the steady flames! Rituals are pillars of belief and cement your faith! If you do not use them daily, you will lose it! Rituals are daily practices, like simple habits! As you repeat them daily, they get glued to your psyche! Repetition is the language of the subconscious! The art of repetition is part of any training! Even master craftsmen, after years of practice, still breathe the oxygen of crucial daily rituals!

You Have Intuition!

What is prayer? What is intuition? It is said that "when you pray, you talk to God!" and "when God talks to you, it is intuition." Almost all human beings have a spiritual need to communicate with the higher power, God! The power of God, no matter how it is known to you, is like the power of a cane to a born-blind man! It elevates your confidence, inspires your spirit, and promotes physical and emotional well-being! Your mind is an incubator of emotions, good and bad! God is an anchor for you to turn to for stability in life! When you talk to God in prayer, it frees up emotions! It gives you the calmness to proceed with your life! Without that recess, your thoughts will lose clarity! Your speech and action will be spiritual orphans! God is our spiritual strength and ultimate refuge where we unleash our wishes, fears, and feelings! Once in a while, we all get a kind of strange intuition! That happens when we are in unison with divinity!

RESPECTING OTHERS!

Why should you respect others? *Respect* means admiring others, appreciating them, and holding them in high esteem! When you respect others, you are respecting you! In the process, it defines you as a caring person when you respect another individual as worthy! You are inviting those qualities into your own self! "What goes around comes around" is the law of karma! It is inviolable and operates without fear or favor! If you want to be respected, you should start respecting others! Appreciate and admire before you command them! Whatever you sow, that alone you shall reap! Start sowing the seeds of respect; sooner or later, you will begin to harvest it, no matter what! And your character will become worthy of praise! Respect includes love, care, and compassion! It is the foundation of an interpersonal relationship! Marital harmony is enshrined in mutual respect! Without it, the world order would perish forever! You are what you think, speak, and repeatedly do! Think respect, speak respect, and act with reverence! Your life will be blessed with harmony and peace! Your ego will be in check and will not run amok! *amuck!*

ow to Heal a Fractured Ego

The ego is an impostor—not a real thing! The ego is an expression of one's own spiritual weakness! The ego is a habit cultivated over time. Start with strengthening your positive traits, like kindness, gratitude, empathy, and compassion; it takes more time to heal a fractured ego! The ego is like a vulnerable limb, inviting frequent chances of fracture! To heal it, cultivate humility, and begin to respect others, no matter who they are! Cultivate an appreciation for everything that you see and everyone who crosses your path! Start loving people for what they are and not what they have! Attend Sunday church service, or visit places of worship! Seek solitude! And reflect on the broader purpose of life! Ask these two questions: *Who am I?* and *Why am I here?* An answer may or may not come! A paradigm shift is the foundation for healing a fractured ego!

The Role of Positive Affirmations in Achieving Goals

Every goal is a deep desire; it makes a track to run on! While wishful thinking is futile, goals are purposeful, just like dreams do not work until you work hard! Goals are ineffective if not backed by sheer work! Every goal backed by emotional support is effective! Positive affirmations give every goal vigor and life! They take goals to the creative incubator hidden in the layers of the subconscious mind! Repetition is the mother of perfection, a trainer of the subconscious mind, a kind of lullaby! These affirmations—when repeated at certain times, like dawn, dusk, and midday—are very effective! Positive affirmations make repeated impressions, harnessing the power of the subconscious mind! Creation itself is the result of logic and emotion, the logical mind cooperating with the deeper mind! Affirmations are messengers of goals to the deeper mind! They help them reach the shores of the subconscious when lodged in the deeper layers of consciousness! They germinate with stunning accuracy, like a miracle!

You ARE A GENIUS!

Want to be a genius? According to the greatest inventor, Thomas Alva Edison, genius is 99 percent working perspiration and 1 percent inspiration! You and I and anybody can be a genius if we are willing to work hard enough to invoke the 1 percent true inspiration for anything! There is a miracle hiding in hard work; it invokes inspiration! Hard work is the mother of all inspirations, and genius is the effect! You cannot help but become a genius if you work hard and pour your emotions and passion into whatever you do! What does a genius do? A genius always takes the road never traveled, facing immense challenges on the way to his or her destination! But he or she does not take no for an answer, clinging like a leech! It is this hard work, this never letting go, that is the secret of genius! You, too, can be a genius; genius is not reserved for certain people! Every genius is made and emerges from humble beginnings!

DON'T MICROMANAGE THE UNIVERSE!

Surrender to the universe! Do not question the intelligence of the universe! It has an all-knowing awareness! Its tentacles are spread far and wide! It can orchestrate anything; nothing is impossible! Understand this truth when you deal with the universe! You have to make an offer to the universe, like at the temple, church, or mosque, the place of worship you visit to uplift yourself! If you are seeking abundance, act as though you have plenty, and start giving to the homeless, charities, your family, et cetera. After you have made your demands of the universe, trust it, understand it, and surrender fully to its amazing intelligence! As you will yourself into submission when you put your cell phone up for charging, let the universe do its work without interference from you! You do not like to be micromanaged; neither does the vast universe! When you trust fully, you will not micromanage or interfere! Learn to trust the universe and its limitless intelligence; you will be blessed with all your lofty dreams and demands!

Our Biggest Challenge

What is our biggest challenge in living our wonderful life? To keep up our enthusiasm and our lifting motivation! One day, we are on top of the world, everything turns gold, and then somebody says something that dents our psyche! This is how we all live our life for the most part, like it or not, but what if we had a technique to keep us inspired all the time? Would you not be willing to pay any price for that? Think about it! Sure, we would have to be fools to let that slip through our fingers! There is a simple technique that will keep you inspired at all times: adopt a silent mission to "inspire the world, one mortal at a time," and live a life of inspiring others! You got it—eureka! I discovered this technique four decades ago while wandering through life! This is the reason for my writing LinkedIn posts to share, and I am blessed to remain inspired because of all of you! Since it is my life's mission, I do this inspiring with the zeal of a missionary! Lo and behold, it works like magic! I am so happy to share this technique with you!

Start Your Dominant Vocabulary Today!

You unconsciously use many words in daily life; they have a domino effect in your life and your fortune! Consciously choose your dominant vocabulary words today! They will be the guideposts of your life and your philosophy! You want to inspire others? Let *inspiration* be one of them! You want to be compassionate? Let *compassion* be one. You want to be grateful? Let *gratitude* be another choice. You want to dream big; let *dream* be a dominant vocabulary word! Once you start consciously using these words, they will seep into your consciousness, and they will become the raw material of your persona—the sum total of your feelings and imaginings of who you are! Your spirit propels your body to navigate the universe!

The Art of Creative Visualization

Whatever you can see with your inner eyes, you get it in life! Life is a just employer; whatever wages you ask of it, it gives you that and no more! You and I are guilty of asking for less because we are unsure! Change your wages! Ask for whatever you want; it shall be granted! If you ask for a penny, life will gladly give it to you, or ask for gold, and you will be surprised when life hands it over to you, no doubt! Of course, you need to back up your demand with hard work! "Ask and you shall receive, seek and you shall find"; it is pure psychology! Creative visualization is not new to us, as we do it daily; we mine new fears and new anxieties! They become reality! Be particular as to what you are seeing with your inner eyes! The subconscious is an obedient servant; do not question you are the master! You are the master of your creation, your dreams or nightmares! Be vigilant as to what you see; it will become your material reality! When you know how to ask, how to dream, and how to visualize, you will spring into action, bold in asking!

The Art of Horizon Writing

Almost all of us gaze at the horizon at sunrise or sunset! Beautiful images get lodged in our consciousness forever! You could start writing your dreams—that big mansion or car, or that big bundle of money, whatever—on the horizon in big letters! It is a great technique to impregnate the subconscious mind! Dream as big as the horizon, and write the dream down on the horizon! Your subjective mind will absorb it like a sponge, for sure! Even before you realize it, it will become a touchable reality! Your subconscious mind is amenable to suggestion, plastic; horizon writing is a way to see your dreams in a big way! Whatever you do to impress your dreams upon your creative mind is good; it will speed up the translation of dreams into a material reality! Dreaming is not an idle exercise; it is an internal creative process! You need to back it up with constant vigil and creative visualization! Do not worry about the possibilities or impossibilities; you just dream! There is no logic in success, only fervent emotion; it will do the job!

How to Resist Your Digital Craving

With the rapid increase in digital devices and gadgets, we are indulging in more and more digital communication under the pretext that it is part of our job. While mobile phones and computers are part of job requirements, other social media outlets are only personal pastimes. Unless and until you are disciplined in the use of these devices, you will be overwhelmed by them, and many times, they do more harm than good. A personal policy for the operation of these gadgets is a necessity in the digital age. Consider the following five suggestions.

1. Keep your cell phone away from you, preferably in another room, for charging! Do not keep it where you sleep.
2. Wait to open personal messages, which are not official communications, at an appropriate time. This personal information can often jam your brain with additional burdens, compromising your ability to focus on the task at hand.
3. Be careful about posting messages on social media, as they can be picked up by outside agencies for their own personal gain.
4. During meetings, put your cell phone on silent mode.
5. Exhibit this restraint to facilitate efficient use of these gadgets, rather than get overwhelmed by them.

ARE YOU A PLAYER ?

Are you a player or a spectator in life? Have you seen the world football match watched by half the world—more than three billion breathing mortals—the unruly crowd going up and down with unmatched excitement, a fervent display of team loyalty and faithful comradery? Would you like to be a player on that team, creating sensations? Life is like a world soccer game, filled with exuberance!

You could be a player in this game of life, making sensations, touching lives, and transforming countless lives one mortal at a time. You do not have to be a Mother Teresa or a Mahatma Gandhi! You can begin where you are! And whatever you do does not matter. Your willingness to make a difference and your ability to respond are all that you need to be a great player in this game we call *life*!

The universe is always looking for players to engage the world! Start your training today; announce to the universe you are ready, and the rest will be handled meticulously, as though preordained!

Start now; being a player is more fun than being a spectator!

BE AWARE, BE IN THE MOMENT!

Are you guilty of unconscious living? We are all guilty of unconscious living sometime or another, as we are sleepwalkers, going through the mental motions! When you are aware of what you are doing at this moment, you are here, enjoying the moment, a player, not a mere spectator! Life is to be lived with joy, and its purpose is to serve others! Your instrument of perception must be sharpened all the time. Just like a knife loses its sharpness with constant use, so does the mind! Sharpen your mind by interacting with a mind sharper than yours! Do not think of your wife—or your husband, for that matter—while at work, nor think of work when you are with your wife or husband! Learn to compartmentalize! Self-talk can help you do this! Talk silently: *I am with my wife. She demands my full attention!* Ask yourself these questions: *Am I enjoying life, or is life enjoying me? Am I aware of this present moment and what I am doing with it?* Understand that "awareness is the messenger of God"! You are in the presence of the divine only when you are aware!

MANAGING YOUR MIND!

Manage your mind! Manage your life! Why is managing your mind pivotal to happiness? Your mind is your prism of perception; it is your window to the universe! You experience life with the help of your mind! Your pain, your suffering, and your mood are dictated by your mind! Mostly, we are not in control of our minds; they have become yo-yos, going hither and thither like planks caught up in the high seas, always at the mercy of other people's whims! Manage your mind; otherwise, somebody will mismanage it for you! That somebody could be your wife or husband, your son or daughter, your boss, or even a stranger on the highway as you are cruising at eighty miles an hour in your brand-new car! Understand this cruelty; start managing your mind now, or else! The quality of thoughts that you entertain dictates your mood, your feelings of happiness, sorrow, agony, and ecstasy! One day, you are very upbeat, and you are on top of the world; the next day, you are like a deflated balloon and cannot lift up! Awareness is the key to enjoying life! Relish every moment, like a hungry man relishing every morsel of rice he eats; he does not know when, if at all, the next meal is coming! So fragile is life that the next moment may or may not be there for you!

PAIN IS PRIVATE!

Stop suffering! Start living! Suffering is caused by your mind and its imagination! It is not real! Suffering is magnified by the imagining mind! You are reliving the pain several times; it is bad for you. Maybe the reason you are doing this is because you want others to sympathize with you! As the enlightened one, the Buddha, said, "Pain is inevitable. Suffering is optional." Physical pain is unavoidable due to physical injury and disease of the organs being part of existence! But augmenting your pain is a useless "augmented reality"! Do not discuss your physical pain with anybody, even those close to you. Say, "My pain is private and confidential—my own pain!" Put a label on all your pains; small or big ones, it does not matter. The moment you do this consciously, your suffering will go away! Your suffering has become a habit! Every habit is a merciless master; when you think about it, it will not go away, like a rogue tenant you have to evict! So start ignoring your thinking about the pain, take medication, and get busy with other things in life, and the suffering will slowly go away! Do not publish your pain to the outside world! Your family is OK, but outside of that, nobody has to know about your physical pain; it is private and confidential, like your private body part! Do not lie down idle, allowing your mind to magnify the pain!

WHEN YOUR MIND IS FROZEN!

Living in the present means accepting that everything in the present moment is here and now; you cannot change it! Almost all of us live in the past, licking old wounds, or imagine the future and entertain fears that do not exist! To live in the present, you must accept everything it brings with it. You can experience the present moment being in it now. You cannot think about it; if you think, it has become the past! When you are in the present, time does not move; it stands still! You are aware of everything that is happening now as is! There is no judgment in the present; there is no imagination! You embrace the present as is, aware of what is timeless! In that timeless moment of existence, you enjoy life totally, devoid of any pain, fear, or suffering, as the mind is frozen!

RESPONSE — ABILITY!

What is responsibility? Responsibility is very
often misunderstood, misconstrued!

It is the ability to respond!
It is the awareness springing into
action.
You respond effectively when you
are in the present moment.
When you are lost in thought,
Your ability to respond to the
present is impaired. Most of
the time we react which is
spontaneous and many times a
useless and harmful exercise!
Remember when you act you
are a master, when you react
you are a slave! Be a master,
remember to respond with
action. It is irresponsible to
react, any fool can react. But
only wise ones can act!

Do You Want To Be A Trustee?

Wanted: A trustee for the universe! There is a need for a trustee in the universe! Read on! You do not need a Wharton MBA or *simple* an IT engineering degree, only a very simply qualification—a willingness to take responsibility! You can be six-foot-two or five-foot-two, man or woman! Responsibility begins with you; you take responsibility for you, your family, your community, your country, and the planet! Once you make an unconditional commitment to be a trustee, the universe will provide all the necessary tools for your function! It is on-the-job training! It is hands-on training by the best trainers! The universe has already lined up those brilliant trainers for you! It is the road not "less traveled" but "never traveled yet," and you have the best opportunity to serve the entire universe!

Start just now; make the commitment to you, your thoughts, your speech, and your actions; and remain open for the orders! Opportunity presents itself in disguise as a big problem indeed! You grab it by its tail; you are Hercules, here to harness the beast! If you trust the universe with your commitment, the universe will trust you with the trusteeship! It is an ironclad commitment; only you are allowed to open the seal to the best opportunity to serve humankind, the universe—a once-in-a-lifetime opportunity!

DESIRES = BUTTERFLIES!

Unfulfilled desires—are they bothering you? Desire is the engine of life! No desire—no life, no thoughts! Desires are not bad; they are the butterflies in our life. They keep us going; they take us to unimaginable new heights! Be grateful to desires; they deserve our applause and praise! Unfulfilled desires could be the cause of your painful misery. Yet if you know how to handle them, they will leave you alone! It is like a breakup: you break up with one desire and go after a more desirable one. Life has to go on. It does not matter what desire it is; you can find a better one to make your life blessed again.

Every human life has a purpose; find your mission in life! Desires are messengers of the mission, not the end of life! Some desires come into your life as boyfriends or girlfriends—nothing more! You may find one that is more compelling to be wedded to and enrich your life, ~~with a passion and dedication to hang on to~~ that will ~~define your life and your life's purpose and carve out your destiny!~~

With a passionate commitment to that one desire, you embark on a mission to change the world!

The Best Way to Handle Rejections in Life

The opposite of rejection is acceptance! When people criticize you, you take it as rejection, and the drama of rejection starts playing in your mind! But even if a person, including your own wife or husband, rejects you outright, just ignore it! It is not worth losing sleep over it. The day you reject yourself, you have a bigger problem; it can threaten your very healthy existence. The same people who reject you today may desire to dance with you tomorrow, when you become successful and famous. I was in life-insurance sales for more than three decades, and a life-insurance salesman is rejected more than any other professional I can think of. Yet I survived my rejections and made a comfortable living out of it. I just ignored the rejections and kept on doing the cold-calling. From my experience, I realized that the people were not rejecting me; it was just bad timing. When I called a second or third time, the same person was in a different state of mind, and I got the appointment to meet with him or her. The human mind is like a river; the river you see now you will not see again. So is the human mind running at the speed of an electric train. It is constantly changing, and even the owner of the mind does not realize this truth!

WHO AM I?

Who do you think you are? A million-dollar question indeed; philosophers and saints and spiritualists have tried to find answers to it and convey them to us! It is as ancient as man himself, who is still groping in the dark, trying to find the answer to this highly loaded question! Why do you think that this question is pivotal to our existence? It opens the very doors of our dreams, endless possibilities! Eating, sleeping, and reproducing, any organism can do very well, but being the best of his creation, we all could do much more! Our progress during the last century was phenomenal, but we have not scratched the surface yet; it is just the beginning! We are still looking for answers to one fundamental question: *How can I be happy, be at peace with others, and stop the killing?* Abundance is the law of nature, yet we have no food to eat; more than a billion people do not know where their next meal is! Once he gets the answer to the basic question of his identity, man could be more compassionate and build a better world!

CONTINUE LIKE A PRO!

There is no loser in this world, only a different experience! If you give up after an experience and throw in the towel, it is a loss! But if you persist and continue, changing your route, you win. In the stock market, we call it an *unrealized loss*; the loss is only on paper! Because it is only on paper you lose, in reality you have no loss, because you continue your efforts, taking different approaches! As Thomas Edison said, "I realized a thousand ways that won't work," and he changed the course of history and invented the light bulb! Do not call anybody a *loser*, even jokingly; you may feel bad after he or she persists and wins whatever he or she set out to accomplish! You will never fail if you never get up from your seat! If you exercise, you can get sore muscles; this is true in life too! You can get financial or entrepreneurial soreness—part of any business—and muster the courage to get up and march toward success! Every experience comes to teach you a lesson; learn it, and continue your task of building the business like a pro!

THE ONE UNIVERSAL LAW!

You are the universe! Act as though you are part of the universe—an integral part! Anything you desire in this life, the universe will make sure it is delivered to you, provided you obey the laws of the universe! Nobody is above these inviolable laws! Whatever you want from the universe, make a small offer! When you smile at a homeless person, you are smiling at the universe! When you kick a can in the street, you are kicking the universe! The universe includes all the organic and inorganic forms, visible and invisible to the naked eye; it excludes none! Think like the universe, speak like the universe, and act like the universe, and you can command anything; it shall be done to you! Anything you give to the universe will come back to you, multiplied several times; this is the law of reciprocity! You have an equal chance of getting anything from the universe as the richest person or the smartest person here on this planet does! Ask yourself this question: *Am I following the law of reciprocity? Am I treating everyone the way the universe will treat them—equally, without fear or favor, just as a mother treats her children?* Sadly, when you are not, your wishes are not fulfilled by the universe!

LIFE IS A TRADE OFF!

Life is a trade-off! Just remember that! Whenever you do something, you are choosing it over something else! You cannot have all things in life; then, you would be in a big mess. The only question you should ask is, ~~Is what I am getting better than what I am giving up?~~ Proceed if the answer is a big yes! When you got married, you gave up your bachelor life! You need to come home— no more playing poker all night! When you became a mother, you sacrificed other things for being with the baby all night! When you got your first job, you could not sleep till eight o'clock! When you remind yourself that life is a trade-off, you are careful, and you do the cost–benefit analysis of doing anything, it makes you more responsible and less frustrated with new things, as you analyze the pros and cons of things. You got that much-desired promotion; with it came more work, more responsibility, and many late evenings! There is absolutely no free lunch in this world; you have a price to pay for everything you want! This is the stark reality of life!

★ "what I am receiving is more precious than what I am giving up."

IGNORANCE OF THE LAW!

You are very fortunate indeed! No matter who you are and where you are going in life, you are undoubtedly fortunate; rejoice that you can do anything! You are part of this universe! The universe is very kind indeed! It has given you the freedom and power to align with the universe! If you understand the laws of the universe and follow them, you will be immensely rewarded; if you oppose them, you will be punished! Whatever you want in life, make a small offering to the universe! It will return it one hundred times or even more, guaranteed! "Wish for others what you wish for yourself" is the ultimate law! If you follow this law, you will have everything you want to have. When you wish misery for others, you have to eat it too. That is the part people find extremely difficult to swallow! The universe is like your mother; when she cooks delicacies, she wants all her children to have them; so does the universe! Ignorance of this law of the universe is the fundamental flaw! We all pay very dearly for that ignorance; we really miss out on this life! The law of reciprocity is an inviolable law of the universe; know it, and you will be blessed with fortunes beyond your imagination! Whatever you give to the universe, it will give it back multiplied! Anything and everything you see is an integral part of the universe!

The Famous "Failures" in the World

The greatest inventor of all time, Thomas Alva Edison, failed—failed miserably—a thousand times before he invented the light bulb! Abraham Lincoln, the author of the immortal Gettysburg Address, failed in many elections before becoming president of the USA! Henry Ford, who was an auto mechanic at age forty, failed to produce the car of his dreams before success embraced him! The famous Wright Brothers had their first plane in the air for only a few seconds! Walt Disney conceived the idea of Mickey Mouse in a garage! The world only knows people after their success; before success, these people paid a very heavy price in terms of frustration, pain, and anguish! But they all had an insatiable passion, they believed in themselves, and after years of agonizing trial and error, they succeeded! Success is a sure thing for those who are willing to fail! These people sacrificed their entire life for the one thing they wanted. Decide on that one thing you want, put all your focus on it, and keep on failing until you succeed; this is how it is done.

PRISONER OF OPINION!

Are you a prisoner of your opinion? We all have a right to our opinions, our viewpoints, but we need to examine those opinions in the light of change! If our opinions are flawed or based on sentiments, we need to change those opinions and move forward with ease! If we cling to our opinions because of egotistical reasons, we become prisoners, self-imprisoned human beings! We see many self-imprisoned persons walking around like nomads; the world will move on and move ahead, leaving them behind! Understand that change is the essential fabric of life. If you have any doubt, look at your baby picture—how cute! But you moved away from that, and you are a fully grown adult; internalize this reality, and shed your worn-out opinion now! People who made great contributions to the world changed! They embraced change, like Mahatma Gandhi and Mother Teresa! Gandhi was a barrister, Mother Teresa a geography teacher! Look at Gautama Buddha—he gave up everything and got enlightened! You may not be a mahatma or Mother Teresa, but you can change; embracing that change, you can make a difference in the world! Develop your potential, do not remain a prisoner of your opinions, shake off that pride, swallow your ego, and be willing to change!

How to Retool Your Mind

We know we have a very mysterious mind with dual functions. We have an objective thinking mind and a subjective obeying mind! Many times, we want to change our attitude and our inhibitions, but we do not have any direction or any schooling for this change! If we have accumulated decades of information just *being*, we need to allow ourselves at least a couple of years to change, not to be! Patience is a fundamental virtue for mind management, and slowly but surely, you can change your mind and persona! Examine the words you use in everyday communication; start changing those words; insert more positive ones! Begin to smile at others, even strangers, with good intentions; read inspirational passages every day for a few minutes! Be childlike and curious to know more and more things; enroll in a gym. If you have not done so yet, it will activate your mind. Spend fifteen minutes every day practicing pin-drop silence, and your mind will usher in a new era of inspiring positivity!

How to Erase Guilt from the Mind

Almost all of us carry guilt with us, in one form or another! Maybe it is the result of an act of commission, or omission. Many guilts are hidden in our past; they surface occasionally to wreck our peace of mind and well-being, to say the least! We need to take them out of the storehouse of the subconscious mind; we can do this by simply writing, in detail, one guilt at a time! Repentance is the only solution for guilt! Feel repentance in your heart; mentally seek the forgiveness of the person whom you hurt! Bringing the person into your presence through a mental drama and seeking his or her forgiveness this way is as effective as the actual event! We are all connected at the spiritual level; this way, the person gets the message, and repeat the process until you feel peace and calmness inside. Once you have repeated this process for each guilt, you are free—free from guilt at last, with very pure intentions! It is the purity of your heart and the integrity of your purpose that will do the job, releasing you from the guilt forever! Anytime you have a problem, the best thing is to take action. Do not postpone; that way, you can solve the problem and move forward! Inaction will only add fuel to your agony! Forgive yourself; forgive others! Repentance is the only solution!

Seven Daily Rituals for Success and Happiness

1. Begin your day with a minute-long prayer of gratitude!
2. Follow your mind when it is disturbed
   by ups and downs of the day!
3. Always expect the best, even when things go wrong!
4. Always act of your own volition; try not to react.
5. Bless everyone, including your adversaries (if you have any).
6. Use words only to uplift and inspire!
7. Slip into sleep with a minute-long gratitude prayer!
Following these rituals will keep your mind fresh
and inspiring. The only way to remain inspired
throughout the day is by inspiring others!

The Best Tribute to Our Parents

Generally, we are very respectful of our parents. We remember their advice, their love, and their affection, and who could forget their sacrifices for our well-being? But those memories begin to fade away after they are gone! Of course, when we have our own families and children, it is not that easy to keep the same relationships with our siblings! But our parents would definitely like for us to love our siblings, keep those relationships close, and remain in constant touch. Many times, family feuds and financial dealings can harm otherwise-smooth relationships between siblings! Maintaining those smooth relationships after our parents are gone is a challenge we always face, and many times, we fail! Just like the creator loves us, his creations, we must love one another! Our parents, even from their graves, would love for us to remain very close. As a matter of fact, the best tribute we can give to our parents is to be in touch with and love our brothers and sisters! Let us forget the family feuds and the financial transactions and be at least on talking terms with our blood relations! It is also our way of living by example for our children, whom we expect to love each other after we are gone!

Give Away Your Smile!

Please give away your smile! It is fun; it is joy! They say you move fewer muscles in your face when you smile than when you frown. Smiling is the easiest way to double your joy in life! Keep smiling; start with your family members! When you smile at a homeless person, you are smiling at the universe! And the universe will reciprocate in kind, with a hundred smiles! You are creating happiness in the world with more smiles—the best way to change the world! Yes, you can be a catalyst! Smile at your boss every day; she or he will feel your warmth, and what more do you want than a smiling, friendly boss? Smile at your wife or husband, and she or he, too, will reciprocate. You've got the world by the tail when your spouse keeps smiling!

Words Are Sharper Than Swords!

Many great speakers have been able to move the world! Using the power of their words, they have swayed public opinion. Words get their power from the emotion you pour into them! Words charged with emotion become sharper than swords! We need to use them with caution, as they can hurt very deeply, and time may not be able to heal the wounds they inflict! Be careful when choosing your words in conversation; they can do more harm than good in the wrong usage. My mother used to tell me that we must use words to uplift and inspire others, and never to put down another human being! We, as parents, have to make sure that our children follow this, teaching them to use words sparingly, only to uplift and inspire! Many times, an uncontrolled tongue dictates our destiny, it is true, as this habit becomes a merciless master, dictating our behavior. As adults, many of us become slaves of our habits, groping in the dark to get rid of the bad habits! Our words become messengers of joy or sorrow, as they stem from good or bad thought processes, ~~and many times, vice versa~~! Words that express joy bring joy, and words that represent sorrow bring tons of sorrow!

Holy Hours!

Why are holy hours holy? In Sanskrit, holy hours are known as *brahma muhurta*; they take place in the early morning, spanning from 1:30 a.m. to 4:30 a.m. Spiritual seekers get up that early to start their meditation and get fully immersed in these holy hours for spiritual practice! Holy hours are significant, as the conscious mind is dormant; this is the time when the subconscious mind is in a state of peak alertness! It is suitable for impregnating the subconscious mind with new ideas, new prayers, and new positive affirmations! During this time, spiritual seekers are seeking spiritual transformation by reprogramming the subconscious mind, the creative power! With no conscious mind to block their new programming, the subconscious mind gets the message; it converts it into reality! These early-morning hours are fit for fast transformation! Our ancient yogis knew this from their own experience, and they started this tradition to train new aspirants, encouraging them to get up early for their spiritual practice! We too can follow the foot steps of our ancestors, and use the holy hours for faster transformation!

The Secret behind Happiness Chasing You

Who says you have to chase happiness? Stop doing that! Let happiness chase you wherever you go, whatever you do! You will feel happy when you harvest pleasant feelings inside you! Select those actions that can trigger pleasant internal feelings! It is true that when you live for yourself, life is utterly miserable! It is also true that when you live for others, it is purely joyful! Then why do you not live for others? Because nobody told you to do that. Starting today, live for others, and see your happiness multiply! Never ask the question, *Why me?* Always ask, *Why not me?* If your wife or husband asks you to do something, do it! If your son or daughter wants you to get something from the store, run for it, because you will harvest tons of happiness. Thinking about *me* and *me alone* is really boring; it ignites agony and insatiable desires, one after another like waves! Live for others, help others, weep for others, and work for others! You will reap inexplicable joy! Is happiness chasing you now?

The Psychology behind Expecting the Best

The psychology behind expecting the best is rooted in the law of attraction—thoughts always attract similar energies! Your expectation is a mental process, stimulating thoughts and releasing thought energy for the universe to process! The universe reciprocates in kind multiple times; reciprocity is law! The universe is intrinsically programmed to give back what it receives! The universe is very impersonal; it simply follows its own law! There is no fear or favor; it is ordained to perform its function. It does not matter who releases what energy; the universe reacts with cunning accuracy! The law of reciprocity is its very nature! When you expect the best, you simply release positive energy; in the creative incubator of the universe, this energy gets multiplied! Against all odds, expect the best, and you will invariably get it! The alternative is not good, and it is not even worth mentioning! Now onward! Program your mind to expect the best always! It may not work at first; repeat it until it becomes second nature. Always remain grateful; it will keep you focused on your goal! Optimism is the oxygen you need to run the engine of life. Expecting the best is optimism in action, applied enthusiasm; it can open many closed doors you never imagined would open for you!

How to Double Your Income

You can easily double your income if you choose to and simply get out of the way so the universe can help you do so! You have to remove *I* from the equation, as it blocks the way! With *I*, there is a parade of limiting beliefs—such as "It cannot be done." Whatever you do for a living, it does not matter; you can double your income if you simply take *ownership interest* and stay focused! It is not your employer who is the cause of your getting ahead; it is your deep-rooted desire, your dedication and willingness! Let your employer enjoy the material-ownership interest; you take the spiritual-ownership interest, and pour your emotion into your work as though you are possessed by the demon of work! Enjoy every moment; do not disclose your intention to anyone! Make it your silent mission to double your income; you can do it. And look at that new income every day at dawn and dusk! The art of visualization is the secret of any accomplishment! This mission to double your income is your brainchild; nurture it with love and affection! If you continue your mission with the zeal of a missionary and the unmatched love of a mother, you will double it for sure! You can do anything you want to do if you put your mind to it! That is the power of desire; "ask and you shall receive" is very true!

Attitude! Gratitude! Spiritude!

Attitude is the attire of your character—it is its outward display!
It is the sum of the tendencies you have accumulated in life.
Your parents, family members, friends, and teachers have all
helped you in accumulating those tendencies! Gratitude is a
grateful attitude, a deep sense of appreciation for all things, big
and small, that the great creator has created! Gratitude is an
add-on to your basic attitude, a personal gift that propels you
to a higher and lofty way of living, wonder, and awe! As you
evolve through life, you could stumble upon the truth—that
you are not this body or mind but pure spirit, awareness! This
understanding that you are the all-knowing awareness puts
you in a nontraditional oneness with everything! The duality
that *you* is different from *me* does not occur, as you feel an
intimate affinity for the universe and its integrity! Once that
ahum vanishes, the ego dissolves itself into oneness, where
there is only bliss—that feeling of the all-knowing spirit!
The lesson to learn: you are the embodiment of the spirit!

THOU SHALL NOT JUDGE OTHERS!

Are you still judging others? If you are still judging others, it is a sure sign of the superego, where you subconsciously want to feel that you are better—better than the other guy or girl—your ego playing a trick. You cannot judge another, because you are not in his or her shoes! Instead of judging another individual, be empathetic! Show him or her that you care—that your praise is really heartfelt! If empathy is listening without judging, judging is a violation—a violation against the other person's self-respect or honor! How many man hours are wasted in this empty exercise of judgment? How many lives are hurt and reputations harmed? Stop judging once and for all, and use that time to compliment and to uplift another human being to find his or her true potential! Forgive yourself for all the judgments you have committed, and seek people's forgiveness for violating their privacy. Embrace the whole of humanity as one close-knit family, connected on this spiritual World Wide Web with pure love!

Thou shall not judge others is a Spiritual Law!

REWRITE YOUR OBITUARY!

Your deeds go beyond your lifetime! "No man is an island" is a true statement! We live and die, and we leave behind not only our family but plenty of our deeds! In life, we may touch many lives, or we may hurt many lives! We may live a selfish life, or we may live a selfless life for others! We may make a difference in this world with our grateful deeds, or we may make a real mess here before we finally kick the bucket! Our memories may make lofty dreams for others to follow, or our memories may make horror stories and nightmares for others! It is up to each one of us to decide while living what we will leave for dear ones and others in society to remember us. Do we want to leave our footprints in the sands of time, or do we want to leave horror stories for sleepless nights? After we are gone, the world remembers us through our deeds! Our family and friends may relish memories of our living days, or they may want to forget us, closing that chapter once and for all! You still have a lot of time left to write a memorable obituary!

The lesson to learn: rewrite your obituary!

When the Student Is Ready, the Teacher Will Appear!

This famous Vedantic thought is meant to uplift humans by teaching them the need to be patient with all parts of life! Many times, we all feel impatient about things not happening, and inordinate delays can throw us into a pit of frustration! Many times, our impatience itself is an impediment, blocking our progress or our ability to move forward with ease! "When the student is ready, the teacher will appear"—we need to carry this mantra on our tongue to remind us to be patient! When overwhelmed by impulsive behaviors blocking us, we need to recite this mantra to calm our mind, to focus freely. When the salesman is ready, the client will appear, for sure! We will be promoted only when we are spiritually ready! "Ready or not, here we come" is not the rule of the universe! Everything has a set time—a time to sow, a time to reap! Our duty is to focus on the task at hand without fear or worry! And the universe will hand over the fruit at the appropriate time!

THE COMPANY YOU KEEP!

You will become the company you keep! How far you go in life will have a lot to do with the company you keep, the people you hang out with on a regular basis! It is said that your friends must be greater than you so that they can teach you good habits and other qualities you lack! You can be friendly with everyone, but your core friends must be more knowledgeable and experienced than you. You can partake of their optimism and their life experience, and they can take you under their wings and help you fly high. Thomas Edison, the greatest inventor of all time, had a few friends, such as Henry Ford, Harvey Firestone, and the like, to hang out with. They used to meet regularly to exchange ideas and thoughts. A good circle of friends is a prerequisite for a brilliant life! Just as you carefully select your spouse, select the friends whom you are going to hang out with for a long time to come! Your friends should be down-to-earth, practical people, sober and ready to come to your rescue at short notice, if required! The lesson to learn: have a few very good friends!

RELEASING ONE'S UNCONDITIONAL LOVE!

Have you started blessing others? This is the first and foremost step toward emotional freedom! We are all slaves of our emotions; they literally control our mood and lead us down ~~paths~~ we later regret having traveled! Free yourself from the onslaught of your emotions by blessing others! You can start with your children; bless them every morning! Continue with your wife or husband and other family members! Take your blessing to the office; in silence, bless your boss and everyone, regardless of who they are or what jobs they do! Almost all of us are victims of our own anger at some point! Fear shows us the drama of our worst nightmares during the day! When will we escape the wrath of despair and despondency in life? When we start blessing others; this frees us from our emotions! The basic foundation of our life and our origin is love only; once you start giving your pure love to others, you will be free! ~~You will understand the emotions that otherwise haunt you; with that understanding, you will master emotional wisdom!~~ WHAT IS BLESSING? Releasing ~~your~~ one's unconditional love to others.

LIVE EVERYDAY AS IT IS YOUR LAST !

Live every day as though it is your last! If you had only one
day to live, what would you do? You would radically change
your priorities—no time to waste! You would make it less of a
priority to fight with another—no gossip—and every moment,
you would engage with something useful! When you live every
day as though it is your last day here, you will develop a sense
of urgency to finish things one by one! You will not need any
training in time management; your stress level will become ~~negative~~ zero
as you enjoy moments! You will not know how to
postpone things or procrastinate! You will fully engage; your
passion for life will be inexplicable! You will act as though you
are a man or woman possessed. You will really make your life
magic, with nothing to complain about! You will start loving
everybody you meet and have no enemies—who wants to keep
an enemy for just one day, the last day of your life? You will be
more compassionate than the Buddha himself, nobler than the
noblest person who ever lived, and more loving than Jesus Christ!
The lesson to learn: try living every day as
though it is your last; you might like it!

The Habit of Blessing

Cultivate a habit of blessing everyone—and everything! It is a divine habit; it can uplift your mood and attitude! You do not need to be a ninety-year-old saint to have the habit of blessing! You do not need to have a long white beard either! The only requirement to bless another person or a thing is pure intentions, devoid of any mortal ulterior motive! Blessing is the art of releasing one's unconditional love to another human being or any organic or inorganic form! Unconditional love gives you the moral authority to bless everyone and everything that crosses your path, including inert matter! Your enemies will become your friends; they will feel the warmth of your love! You will develop a compassionate personality of your own! All your problems will become easier to solve than before; you will go through a personal transformation, a paradigm shift! This is the fastest way to change; your contentment will soar! You will begin to relish every moment of your life on earth! The lesson to learn: you can bless everyone and everything!

REJOICE IN THE SUCCESS,
WHEREVER YOU SEE IT!

Do you rejoice in the success and happiness of others? You have
to rejoice in others' success and happiness! It is a vital trait for
your own success—your own happiness! We are all connected
by the universal spiritual web, so when you hate another person,
you are hating yourself! When you rejoice in the success and
happiness of other people, you are allowing the same feeling to
flow into yourself! This makes the process of your own success
smooth, easy! Cultivate the habit of joining in the success of others!
Almost all successful people do not hold grudges against anybody,
and they are happy to see more successful people! We create
our own impediments with traces of negativity! These could be
holding you back from your own success! Starting today, rejoice
in the success and happiness of others! And see for yourself the
harmony that you feel within! When you rejoice in others' success
and happiness, you become more proactive; you are cool inside
and ready to usher in your own day of success and happiness!
The lesson to learn: be proactive, and
welcome other people's success!

Dangers of Gossiping

Generally, *gossip* is meaningless conversation about other people, their private lives, and unsubstantiated rumors. Mostly, it involves nothing positive about other people. It is loose talk, intended to be a pastime or time killer. Look at the five dangers of gossip.

1. Almost all gossip is mired in negativity. There is nothing positive about it. You are not praising other people when you gossip.

2. When you gossip, your tendency to engage in negative conversation increases, and eventually, you become a victim of negative conversation. Negative talk eventually becomes a habit, tough to shake off!

3. Whatever negative qualities of other people you discuss during this conversation take root in your conscious mind and subconscious mind. Your mind becomes a breeding ground for negativity.

4. In the long run, if you continue to gossip, you will become a toxic garbage site, and this will lead to mental and physical ailments. No kidding!

5. Even if you want to pull out of this idle conversation, you may not be able to do so easily, as other negativity-mongers will entrap you in this chronic habit.

The lesson to learn: Stay away from negative talk. This habit is a merciless master; you may not be able to stop it once you start!

How to Transcend Your Belief System

We all carry a bundle of beliefs from our childhood. Some of them we accumulated on our way through different phases of life. If we dissect our belief system, we will notice it carries suggestions our parents implanted in us while we were little kids. Some suggestions were planted by other close family members, like our brothers and sisters and uncles and aunts. Over a period of time, our subconscious mind picked up those suggestions as truths, and we became our beliefs. Now, to change our belief system, we need to implant new suggestions into our conscious mind—and, more important, into our subconscious mind. Positive affirmations are the best tools to reprogram our subconscious mind. We must feed those positive affirmations to our subjective mind at dawn and dusk, when our conscious mind is in a semiwaking state. Tell yourself, *Every day in every way, I am getting better and better!* and *I am increasing my sales every day!*—see those possibilities before your mind's eye. You can put a dollar sign there and see it as a present possibility. Make your own positive affirmations. Take one suggestion at a time, and practice it for ninety days. Over a period of one to two years, you will become a believer in your ability to change!

The Story of Ratnakar

A long time ago, in a small village in India, there lived a robber named Ratnakar! He used to rob people of their valuables! The villagers stayed away from him, knowing his behavior! His victims were strangers who happened to pass through! One day, a highly venerable saint was passing through the village, and Ratnakar approached him to take away his valuables. "Why are you doing this?" asked the saint. "To support my family." "Do you know you alone will suffer for your sin, not your wife?" Ratnakar said, "No way. My wife will also suffer." The saint laughed! "Please go home, and ask your wife. I will wait," said the saint. Ratnakar ran home in order to know if his wife would partake in his sin, and after a few minutes, he returned with a guilty look. "What happened?" asked the saint. "My wife said she is not responsible for my sins. 'You alone suffer for what you do,' she told me." It was a revelation for the wayside robber; he fell to his knees. "Forgive me," he lamented. "Please accept me as your disciple." The saint was kind enough to offer him spiritual refuge. Thus, Ratnakar spent years in severe penances, and he became Saint Valmiki, who wrote the great epic *Ramayana*, the story of Rama! Even a sinner can become a saint with personal transformation!

Love at First Sight

We hear about love at first sight; maybe you have experienced it too! There is a magic hiding in love at first sight! When a boy and girl are attracted to each other, an avalanche of emotion pours out there! Emotion is the glue that sticks anything to our spirit! Innate to the nature of humankind is an indestructible spirit! Because of the outpouring of emotion, the love becomes eternal, making it hard to separate those two romantic souls from each other! The same occurs when you pour emotion into any goal that you set; no force can separate you and the goal from each other! You become, in a matter of speaking, romantically made for each other! And your successful attainment of your goal becomes reality! This is the power of emotion, which you can apply to your goal! Emotion is the programming language of the subconscious! It is the creative incubator of man, where dreams come true! Soak your goals in emotions; see them bear fruits for sure! The lesson to learn: emotion is the key to the attainment of goals!

Destination Unknown

Life is a journey of dreams from the cradle to the graveyard!
Humans are lonely travelers, many times not knowing the next step.
Many people join this journey, but one by one, they all leave, hoping
against hope they continue to *destination unknown*! Reminding
ourselves always about this unknown destination heals; almost all
our hearts break as we land on the plane of reality! Only fools can
think that life is permanent—that we own everything! Ownership,
of course, is a myth, as our bodies, too, are borrowed! Alas, we
are all chasing a rainbow, stepping on many toes; how many lives
are hurt in our attempts to get ahead? No matter who we are and
what our accomplishments are, we all end up in a six-foot box for
the final journey! Knowing that our greedy journey is futile should
open our eyes, and helping one another, hurting none, we can find
a little joy! This truth that we are all here for a short visit must
stick; our purpose is to love one another before kicking the bucket!
The point to ponder: is life real?

How to Quiet a Restless Mind

The mind is our instrument of perception! We see and experience the world through the prism of our seeing minds, our inner eyes! When our minds are restless, our vision blurs, and we see our universe distorted, shattered into pieces! We need to watch our state of mind like a guard, not allowing intruding thoughts to take a seat in our minds! Our minds are the sum total of our thoughts that are present at any time! When we look at a thought, it flees from the shores of our mind! When the mind is not engaged, we need to anchor it; for sure, we need to have an anchor thought, a mantra, to constantly engage it! The mind has an inborn tendency to dwell on negative thoughts! The anchor thought can divert our mind to positive ones! A mind left unattended is like a child left unattended for a while! It can cause tension and turmoil and get out of control! Mind management is an art; practice it daily to save your sanity! Feed the mind with thoughts of love, kindness, and compassion! Whatever message you paint on the canvas of your mind dictates your personality; you can be a saint or a poor sinner! The lesson to learn: do not leave your mind unattended!

Choosing Kindness as a Ritual

You are unique one of a kind!
kindness is the song of your mind
An ounce of kindness is better than
gold
It is better than any story untold!
Life is a parade of kindness
Starting from your mother,

A kind heart is better than twenty
four carat gold. It can penetrate
even the hardest rock in the world.
Try to practice kindness, it can take
you to places you never imagined.
kindness is your passport to
peace and plenty. It will open
doors to spiritual upliftment and
pure awareness. Practice of kindness
everyday as a ritual is the best
way to enhance your quality of life!

The Psychology behind Awards

The human mind can get into a rut of lethargy and inertia!
Keeping it alive and awake at all times is no laughing matter!
When you are down and things are not at all going well, you
have to consciously reactivate your mental faculties! Looking at
your past achievements, awards, successes, and diplomas will
ignite you, energize you, and remind you that you are a real
winner! Inspired by these thoughts, you will be ready to jump in
to win again! In ancient times when kings ruled, there were huge
halls where artists, especially female artists, performed dances
praising the king and his various attributes and qualities! Really,
these were exercises to activate and stimulate the king's mind!
We all get into inactive modes, and we need to stimulate our
minds too! We should keep our minds focused through regular
exercise; also, watching different sports and super ball reminds
us of winning and inspires us to move forward in the process!
The lesson to learn: keep your mind stimulated!

DEVELOP YOUR INTUITION!

Do you have an intuition? Check it out! We all have a subconscious mind, the seat of emotions! All paranormal activities, such as intuition, are normal traits! In many people, intuition is predominant, and in others, it is dormant! But you have the ability to nurture yours if you choose to do so! Remember your subconscious mind is your subjective mind! Capable of seeing without eyes, it can read what's inside sealed envelopes! It can read others' minds, and it can move objects—you name it! The purer your intentions, the better your chances of developing your intuition! When you think of good things happening to others, keep it a secret, and watch the outcome; you will be amazed at the accuracy! You are intuitive! Intuition is a dormant faculty; you can activate it! Having pure intentions, our mothers have very good intuitions! The lesson to learn: you can develop your intuition!

"The cow on the paper does not eat grass!" my mother used to tell me when I was a teenager. "Gopi, remember the cow on the paper does not eat grass!" This saying was too deep for a teenager; I did not quite get it. Yet I knew there was deep-rooted wisdom hiding in it. After I became a stockbroker, I got involved with using graphs, pictures, and other performance displays to highlight the market! When I was using these graphs and charts, I was reminded of my mother's words: an imaginary cow does not eat grass! I found that this saying also represents the vast difference between theory and practice! Anybody can put a cow on paper; the cow is just imaginary. In real life, do not get carried away by pictures and graphs. They do not depict reality; they are merely the cow on the paper!

The lesson to learn: Ask this question—*Is the cow real?*

MONEY IS GOOD!

Is money the root of all evils? Money is *not* the root of all evils! Money is very good! As long as it brings joy to others, it is a valuable resource! Like any other resource, if it is used to the detriment of another, it can create painful consequences, producing evil results! But money can do wonders in this world; it can change the world—reduce poverty, reduce diseases, plant trees, and build schools! Billionaires such as Gates and Buffett have proved that money is good, and they use it to uplift humankind everywhere! But in the wrong hands, money could be the root of all evils! Love of money to the exclusion of everything else is harmful! Money is a symbol of prosperity, abundance, and wealth! The Hindus worship wealth as the goddess Lakshmi! Accumulate more wealth; work hard; invest well; exploit none! You too can join the ranks of wealthy people who change the world! Do not shun wealth, saying, "It is the root of all evils in the world!" Remember, money is good as long as it brings joy to others! The lesson to learn: money is good.

Practice Gratitude

Maximize your happiness by practicing gratitude! Practicing
gratitude is a way of life; it is a mindset! When you practice
gratitude, you are not just saying thank you for favors received!
Gratitude is the spiritual art of appreciating everything and
everyone for whatever they are! It is empathy in action! Gratitude
must be your only attitude in life, no matter what! Even when
tragedies strike and misfortunes fall, be grateful; it could be ~have been~
worse! Every experience is a great teacher—a teacher who cannot
be found in Harvard or MIT or U of C! When you navigate
through life with sharply grateful eyes, you see the wonders
of the universe hiding there! Your perception gets magnified,
your mind very much focused! Practicing gratitude is loving,
caring for, and sharing with the world around you! Think of
a life where you are free of haunting negativity! Your mind
expands, breaking walls of limitations! You become an eagle,
soaring into peace! When you are at peace, even heaven is not
attractive! Practice gratitude; maximize your happiness!

Solomon's Wisdom

Solomon is said to have been famous for his wisdom and intellect!
He had a keen sense of justice; he was well known for this! One
day, two women came to his court, crying and weeping, and one
of the crying women carried a baby in her arms! Both claimed
the motherhood of that baby, mercilessly accusing the other of
trying to snatch her child away! Solomon asked each mother to
put her case before him; stopping the accusation of the other, he
would reach the decision! Each woman put forward her case in
the hope of winning! The wise king heard both the women and
said in a stern voice, "It appears that the child belongs to each
of you." He asked for one of his soldiers to cut the child into two
halves, one for each woman! The drama intensified when the
soldier appeared on the scene! With a sword in his hand, he was
about to cut the baby in two! But one woman jumped in front of
the baby and yelled sobbingly, "Let her have my baby! I do not
want my baby killed!" King Solomon rose from his throne, took
the baby, and handed it over to the woman who wanted the baby
to live! The wise king knew no mother would wish her child to be
harmed, let alone killed! His keen intellect was on display here!
The lesson to learn: love never hurts!

Stop Worrying! Start Living!

Stop worrying, and start living your life! It is time! Problems are like waves in the sea—as one set crashes at the shore, another one is forming below the horizon! What is the point in worrying? Face challenges as they come! But don't start barking now, thinking that you will be a dog not in this life but in the next life! It is ludicrous thinking! The future is filled with wild imaginations—*What if? What if!* Stop imagining, start living today, get engaged, and be passionate! Today is the joy; yesterday is the pain, licking old wounds! The future is filled with gripping fears! Let them drown in the sea! Once you start living, your worries will no longer haunt you! You will begin to enjoy everything life has to offer, for sure!

The lesson to learn: start living, and worries will go away!

The Journey of a Thousand Miles ...

"The journey of a thousand miles begins with a single step," says
a Chinese proverb—a great lesson for all of us to take in! Today,
you can take the first step to get rid of a bad habit! Today, you can
take the first step by registering at a gym! Today, you can take the
first step by enrolling for your MBA! Today, you can take the first
step by starting a gratitude journal! Today, you can take the first
step by starting a new diet! Today, you can take the first step by
cleaning your office! Today, you can take the first step by reading
a story to your child! Today, you can take the first step by helping
your wife with dishes! Today, you can take the first step to learn
a new skill! Celebrate the Chinese proverb; take that first step!

Seeing God in Everyone ...

Seeing God in everyone is the highest philosophy! It is more than
a philosophy; it is an applied philosophy! A person has nothing
more to attain in the world than this! With it, he or she is blessed
with an all-knowing awareness! The only question for you is this:
Can you see God in everyone? It is not that easy; when emotions
run high, you feel stressed! It is a challenge, but at least take up
the Herculean task of seeing God in one person at a time! If you
fail, that is OK too! It is in the nature of your mind to expand;
if you keep on trying, sooner or later, you will have success! You
will shout, "Eureka!" Ruling out the possibility with excuses is
not the way to go! It will only add more doubts, more reasons
to accept excuses! If you cannot see God in every person, try
the reverse—try to see everyone in God every time you pray!
Do not be afraid to fail; after many failures, you will succeed!
That will be your eureka moment—success at last after many
trials! Seeing God in everyone is the ultimate goal for humans!

CLEAN up YoUR THoUGHTS!

Can you run away from yourself? Of course not! You carry your mind and memories! Wherever you are, they follow you like a loyal shadow! You can run away from your family, your friends, and the world, but never from you and your accumulated haunting thoughts! Understand this radical truth, and clean up your thoughts! A clean mind is your best asset for living in this world! Money helps, family helps, a good job helps, but to enjoy everything, you need a clean and focused mind. It is your passport to the world of joy and happiness! "Where is happiness for a person not at peace with himself?" asks the *Bhagavad Gita*, one of the Hindu scriptures! Engage in calming thoughts, inspiring words, and uplifting deeds, and you can have a clean mind, ready and willing to obey!

To do: clean your thoughts daily!

IS DEATH THE END?

Is death the end of life? Death is the end of life if we think we are our body, because that body is cremated or buried when we die! The question is, *Who are we—this perishable body or mind, or something that we cannot see that has become us?* After I die, my son will say, "My dad's body is lying in state!" What happened to Gopinathan Nair, the so loved "dad"? Where did he go? Who was he? Unanswerable questions! They imply that Gopinathan Nair was not his body! Death is not the end of life; it is the end of a life cycle, just as we discard old clothes and put on new clothes, as the *Bhagavad Gita* describes death and transformation! The soul abandons the dilapidated body in search of a new one! Thus, understanding the nature of human life, our eternal duty, can pave the way for a harmonious life while in this body, knowing full well that we could reappear in another body with all the tendencies we have accumulated here and before! Should we mourn death? Celebrate the life of the departed? All of us will have to give up our borrowed body and depart in search of a new body, or go back to our origin, resting in the ocean of consciousness, never to return again! Ask this question: *Who am I?*

PURPOSE OF LIFE!

Are you very happy today? If not, ask yourself why. What kinds of thoughts are you thinking? Are they negativity-coated or positivity-coated? Check them out! The amount of happiness you derive in this world is directly equal to the amount of happiness you are willing to give others! The universe is a just capitalist! It gives you back what you give it! The farmer knows how the law of reciprocity operates! The law of reciprocity is an inviolable universal law! It says the universe will give back whatever you give it and multiply it multiple times! Now that you know the secret of happiness, be a kind distributor; give to one and all nothing but your smile and kind words! Make sure your thoughts are coated in positivity, ready to uplift! Never judge another; you do not know what he or she is going through! Life is a journey from the cradle to the graveyard! Expect the best! Touch lives on your way; you may not see them again! Anybody can eat, sleep, and reproduce, but you can do better! Make a big difference! Touch lives, leaving happy memories! Ask this question: *What is the purpose of life?*

START NEW THINGS!

Are you breathing? Give yourself a pat on your back! Many people are not so fortunate! They went to sleep last night and did not open their eyes today! So you are one of the fortunate ones! Celebrate life today! You can face your problems and challenges with the right attitude! "I had my blues because I had no shoes, until on the street I saw a man who had no feet"—how trivial our challenges are! Start every day with an *I can* attitude; never give up! You were made in the image and likeness of almighty God! It is never too late to start something new! You are very young! Your functional age is a state of mind, not a calendar date! Your brain is capable of accepting any challenge, new thoughts, new ideas, and a new vision; it can handle all very well! Today is the first day of the rest of your life; start something! It can challenge you and bring the best out of you! Read a new book, learn a new skill, or even find romantic love! Who says it cannot be done? Look at the tremendous possibilities! If you do not use your brain, you will lose it!

Do Not Bite, but You Can Hiss!

In a tropical Indian village, there lived a poisonous serpent who was very mean and dangerous! Villagers were really scared of him! During the day, little children were scared to pass by his area; with great difficulty, they crossed the bushy area with their parents. One day, a *sanyasi* (monk) was passing through the village, and the villagers complained to him about the snake! The monk went to the nest of the snake, subdued the serpent, and gave him a mantra to think of God and do no harm! With this, the snake became docile and did no harm anymore! When the village boys came to know of the snake's change of heart, they started pelting stones at the snake, being very mean to him! The snake grew very thin, as he could not come out of his hole.

After a few months had passed, the monk came back to the village, and the boys said that the snake was now very good, not harming anyone! The monk was pleased! As he reached the hole and saw the snake, he could not believe his eyes, as the snake was a skeleton—about to die! Then the monk touched him to bring him back to life, and the snake said, "I did as you asked; I was docile. But kids started harming me." The monk felt very sorry for the snake, and he said, "I asked you not to bite! I did not ask you not to hiss!" Do no harm! You can hiss to protect yourself!

Empathy is the foundation of diversity and inclusion! Now, we are debating the need to understand diversity, talking about more inclusive policies and practices at work! This awareness is good, and the debate is good, but our focus must be on individual awareness and the practices of a culture of empathy! An HR manual that mentions diversity and inclusion only provides lip service; it has no teeth! What is *empathy*? It involves listening without judgment and with a keen interest to understand people who come from different backgrounds! Empathy is a personal trait, not a corporate logo! Getting people involved in day-to-day interactions is the answer to building empathy! Having a culture of empathy and compassion at all corporate levels, and celebrating diversity at the grassroots level, could help! Training in diversity and inclusion must start in schools, and students must get to know the meaning and spirit of diversity! America has become the melting pot of the world! It attracts the best talent in the world; diversity is a national necessity!

The action to take: cultivate empathy!

There Are No Underachievers!

There are no *underachievers*; this label is just a judgment call! No one has the right to judge another individual! Nobody can step into another person's spiritual and emotional shoes! That person alone is privy to his or her situation, so stop calling people names! You should not be in the business of labeling people based on your opinions—*overachievers, underachievers; good, bad*; et cetera. If you can do anything, be empathetic and caring to everyone, rather than diffusing their enthusiasm by labeling them. People can turn out to reach their best, even at the last moment, if you have the patience and willingness to wait! Labeling others is your ego playing a trick on you, thinking that when others underachieve, you are an overachiever!

POWER OF TONGUE!

Your tongue is your most valuable business tool! In this ever-evolving digital world of blockchain tech and AI, it is paradoxical how important your tongue, a physical organ, is! All your negotiations at the corporate level, or personal level, rely on your ability to convince others of your viewpoint! Your tongue can make or break a very sensitive business negotiation! It can spoil a billion-dollar deal if your tongue is too sharp! Yet the same tongue can save a merger or an acquisition if the tongue is restrained! Some people have developed a knack for using their tongue at the right time, and others foolishly misuse theirs. Your tongue is the most important ally in your negotiations at home with your children or at the corporate level!

There Will Be Rain after Thunder!

The Greek philosopher Socrates used to get lost in thought, brooding over the nature of the universe and the purpose of life! He was way ahead of his time and his peers at a time when Greece was a progressive civilization! It is said that Socrates had a very lovely, demanding wife, and one day, as Socrates was sitting immersed in his thoughts, his wife came and asked him something repeatedly! He did not hear, as his head was entertaining other thoughts! It is true that women do not like it when somebody is ignoring them, and Socrates appeared to be completely ignoring his wife! So she lost her patience, lifted a pot of drinking water, and mercilessly broke it over the philosopher's head! The philosopher slowly opened his eyes and saw his wife! "I knew there will be rain after thunder," said the philosopher! The lesson to learn: a sense of humor can save your skin!

Your Attitude Dictates Your Altitude!

Your attitude is everything; it is the attire of your character! You change your attitude, and you change the direction of your life! A grateful attitude is *gratitude*; it has its own magical touch! In gratitude, there are only winners; the giver and the receiver both win! Your attitude forms based on your upbringing at home, your education, and of course the company you keep! If you have taken decades to form your current attitude, you must allow yourself at least a few months to change that attitude! Cultivate a grateful mental attitude, or GMA; it can jump-start your life and your career and change your inner wiring! Gratitude is a game changer in life; it erases negativity, leading you to the royal path of freedom from fear and anger! Where you go with your life is based on how you look at it—your attitude, your interactions with others, and your outlook! Your outlook is a reflection of your inlook! What is going on inside? If you learn to appreciate everything and everyone, you will go places! Changing your attitude will transform your life!

The Story of the Donkey-Lion

A long, long time ago, there lived a washerman in a small village! At sunrise, he would leave the village with his herd of donkeys and go to the forest, where there was a stream to wash the clothes, and the donkeys would carry the villagers' clothes back and forth from the forest! One day, when they came back from the forest, the washerman's wife noticed a lion cub, and his children wanted to keep it! So the cub grew up with the donkeys and helped the washerman. Slowly, the cub became a fully grown male lion, the king of the forest! One day, when the donkeys and the lion were resting in the forest, another lion saw this donkey-lion and was dumbfounded! When the donkey-lion was alone, the lion came to him and asked, "My friend, what happened to you? You are a lion! What are you doing with these stupid donkeys? It is absurd!" The donkey-lion said, "I am working for my master; he feeds me." The lion continued, "You are a lion, the royal king of the jungle! You are wasting your life with these stupid creatures! Look at me; I am like you. But the donkeys are not like you. Go to the water, and see your image, and then believe me." The donkey-lion did just that, and he realized he was different! At that, he put his foot down and roared! The donkeys ran for their lives! *Wake up, and roar!*

How to Heal a Broken Spirit

Broken bones and a broken spirit take a long time to heal—more so a broken spirit, as it is invisible to X-rays! When you fall or are assaulted, bones are fractured! But no spiritual fall or person can assault your spirit! Your spirit breaks when you have a constant emotional leak! This can be caused by the sudden loss of a loved one or a tragedy that makes life seemingly impossible to continue, for now! An emotional leak happens when the mind is filled with the darkness of ignorance! Heavy financial losses, the loss of one's personal reputation, or a fall—all these can cause a person to lose emotional strength! Despair is a fatal poison that causes a person's spiritual death! When you feel despair, assemble loved ones around you to infuse you with fresh spirit! Oftentimes, constant weeping and crying is a way to let go! Go through the process, and get out of denial—the crucial stage! Friends and family members with strong spiritual reserves can help you get through the tough time of an emotional leak! Engage in monotonous tasks to reassemble your shattered mind! Religious rituals and prayers with family members both will help! Of course, you can make the determination to come out of the leaking hole, and with the help of healing time, your broken spirit will heal! But you must go through the process!

You HAVE A CHOICE!

He

Do you blame God for anything? God gave you the power of discrimination, the right to choose! The choices that you make create your destiny; He does not! We can fall and falter many times; do not blame God for that! You consciously make choices and make changes to your plan! Look at a baby as it learns to walk: It falls many times a day, but it gathers the courage to get up and walk again with a smile! The little baby even knows instinctively to make adjustments! The baby does not blame God, not even its parents, who are there! We all have something to learn from the baby. Do your part! Falling is part of walking; complete the other part—getting up! Do not blame God or your parents, or anybody for that matter. "Child is the father of man"—the poet really knew his philosophy! If your choices are wrong, you can correct them with new ones; it is your willingness to fail that makes you a successful person! It is dangerous to play the blame game! It derails your focus; it wastes your energy! Conserve every bit of energy to move forward! The lesson to learn: You have choices. Choose another good one!

RESPECT MATHEMATICS!

Did you respect mathematics in high school? I did not respect mathematics in high school, and I got poor grades! If you did respect it, I am sure you were a good math student! It is the law of the universe: it reciprocates in kind! If you love somebody, he or she will love you! With hate, hate you get! Can you tell this to your high schooler?: "Respect mathematics, and mathematics will respect you!" This is as true as daylight! When you respect, pay attention to, and adore someone, the universe will reciprocate in kind, several times! This is the law of attraction! You attract that which you think! If you ridicule, ridicule will come back to you in an avalanche! Understanding the law of reciprocity is a great lesson for all—you, me, children, adults, and every breathing soul around!

The lesson to learn: respect mathematics,
and mathematics will respect you!

Tomorrow May Never Come!
Today Is Already Here!

Almost all of us, me included, try to postpone things! *Tomorrow, I will be happy after I get that new job! Tomorrow, I will go see my mother or father! Tomorrow, after my blood test, I will get life insurance!* The fact is that for many people, that tomorrow did not come! They did not become happy or see their mother or father! It was too late for them to get life insurance! Understand this reality of life: life pulsates in the present! Today, you can go embrace your lovely wife or husband! Today, you can kiss your child and say a kind word to your boss! Tomorrow, it may be too late! No need to shed tears—too bad! You live in the present moment, you enjoy the present moment! If you are alive, you can repeat the joy again tomorrow! Do not postpone your life; you may not have it tomorrow! Life will blossom with joy and happiness when you live in the present! Your wife or husband will thank you for the embrace and your heavenly bliss!

The action to take: do today what you can!

DON'T BE IMPATIENT!

Are you impatient? "For all good things in life, you have to wait," Mother used to say. Something that is readily available may not be good! When you get your food fast in a restaurant, it may be three days old, but at home, you wait when your wife makes food fresh for you! Impatience is a mental weakness, your ego on display! It says to others, "I am an important person! I don't have to wait; let others wait!" It is true that for all good things in life, you have to wait, and wait. How long did you wait to get married—to be a father or mother? At eighteen, you can have a child fast, but what price will you pay? And your innocent child will pay! There is a bliss in waiting, and there is a purpose in waiting; understand that! When you are no longer impatient, you will enjoy life. I am constantly reminded of what my mother used to say, and it empowers me and inspires me to wait for anything in life! Every wait emboldens you and makes you spiritually strong to go forward! Impatience grants you hypertension and a miserable habit. Do not swallow your food right away, unless you have a toothache! Take time to chew it; make it a paste before swallowing it! You have to experience every aspect of life; this is the joy! Waiting is also a joyful experience, once you understand it! Don't be impatient.

WATCH YOUR ANGER!

Are you in control of your anger? Anger is perhaps the most violent negative emotion! It can play havoc in your personal life and family life. Anger is also probably the least understood emotion, as it is hushed up in the secrecy of one's family quarters! I have observed that when a person is angry at somebody, he or she is angry at him- or herself for an act of commission or omission! The other person just so happens to be the victim of the angry outburst! Anger is like any other habit; it becomes a merciless master! Anger has three stages: thought, speech, and action! It is easiest to control when it is at the thought stage; when it crosses the speech stage, it is beyond controlling! Understanding that you are vulnerable to anger can help! Then you can take corrective action when your anger is at the thought stage—go into your prayer room, close the door, and sit quietly! Or you can walk away from the scene and go to the park; changing your scenery is a very effective method for curbing it! You can dissect the cause of your anger too; it may not be as bad as you thought after all! Learn to forgive yourself and forgive others—it is a good remedy! It is also a long-term cure for chronic anger—very practical! The action to take: watch your anger when it begins!

How to Handle Parental Conflicts

Parenting is a never-ending task of learning on the job! It seems to be a work-in-progress, trial-and-error method! After four decades, I am still learning, like a kindergarten boy! But I would like to share some of my thoughts, as they may be helpful! As parents, we are merely temporary custodians of our children! We do not own them; we can only guide them if they permit us! We notice more conflicts once our children are teenagers; boys and girls are equally challenging when it comes to conflicts! Appreciate them when they question you; they are thinking adults! Tap into your emotional wisdom when dealing with parental conflicts! Never engage in a shouting match; you will surely lose! Try to listen to your children without judging them; show absolute empathy! Never compare your children with others; everyone is unique! Never bring up past actions and failures; they are now history! When emotions run high, resort to silence; shut your mouth! Never threaten teenagers by withholding money or allowances! The teenage years will pass; they will come to their senses! One day, they will become parents, and they will respect you! Parental conflict is natural; love your children for who they are! If your emotions overwhelm you, remember this too shall pass! The action to take: bless your children always!

The Power of Initiative

Initiative has its own built-in power—a power to seek, a power to ask, and a power to make an all-knowing knock! Having initiative means doing something without being told to do so—a person does something of his or her own volition, with no pressure! Initiative is a trait needed for success, and anybody can cultivate it. You may see a number of people who are less smart than you and may not even hold a college degree but are doing better than you! It is the power of initiative that makes high school dropouts succeed in business, industry, or any field they choose! *Initiative* is another word for industry, passion, or drive! Those who have initiative seem to be possessed; they cannot let go of their desire! It does not matter who you are and where you are going! Cultivating the habit of initiative can jump-start your success! It can transcend many of your shortcomings, like education, smartness, and family background, and put you in the forefront! The action to take: start cultivating initiative. Bill Gates, Steve Jones and Zuckerberg are some of the giants in taking the initiative!

RECYCLE YOUR THOUGHTS!

Are your thoughts getting old? If you are thinking about the same things that you thought about ten years ago, your thoughts have become stagnant and outdated! Since you are what you think, you are really outdated and old! Develop the curiosity of a child and childlike behavior to refresh! New thoughts come from new knowledge and new associations, and your curiosity to know new things will take you places you have never imagined! And every day will pose new challenges for you! This is how we create new thoughts and add vitality to our lives! The books that you read, the courses you take, and the friends you have all will contribute to the quality of your everyday life! Whenever you feel life has become the same old same old, have a shift in perspective; make new friends, read new books, and harvest fresh, new thoughts! It is important that we keep the vitality in our thinking, as we are the end results of our thoughts, the seeds of life! A young mind alone can create a young body and youthful health! Recycle your old thoughts, and sanitize them with vigor and vitality!

TELLING LIES!

Can we live without telling lies? This is a million-dollar question disrupting the peace of many independent thinkers and genuine people! I ask this question every day of my life and try to limit my lies! It is hard! I try to limit them to white lies—lies that do not hurt another mortal—as much as possible and deliberately try to tell the truth as much as possible! But to my surprise, a special development is taking place! I am not facing too many situations where I have to tell lies! My take on this development is that the universe will spare you if your intentions are pure and you really do not want to hurt anyone! So be aware of the need to tell the truth! And as much as possible, tell the truth, barring a few white lies! As you pursue your intention of telling the truth, you invite like-minded people and circumstances into your life! Your thinking creates those circumstances, and those circumstances are the offspring of your thoughts!

CPSIA information can be obtained
at www.ICGtesting.com
Printed in the USA
LVHW092142060221
678613LV00034B/248